Numerology for Beginners

An Essential Guide to Numbers and Their Meanings, Divination, and Astrology

© Copyright 2022 - All rights reserved.

The contents of this book may not be reproduced, duplicated, or transmitted without direct written permission from the author.

Under no circumstances will any legal responsibility or blame be held against the publisher for any reparation, damages, or monetary loss due to the information herein, either directly or indirectly.

Legal Notice:

This book is copyright protected. This is only for personal use. You cannot amend, distribute, sell, use, quote, or paraphrase any part or the content within this book without the consent of the author.

Disclaimer Notice:

Please note the information contained within this document is for educational and entertainment purposes only. Every attempt has been made to provide accurate, up-to-date, and reliable, complete information. No warranties of any kind are expressed or implied. Readers acknowledge that the author is not engaging in the rendering of legal, financial, medical, or professional advice. The content of this book has been derived from various sources. Please consult a licensed professional before attempting any techniques outlined in this book.

By reading this document, the reader agrees that under no circumstances is the author responsible for any losses, direct or indirect, which are incurred as a result of the use of the information contained within this document, including, but not limited to, errors, omissions, or inaccuracies.

Free limited time bonus

Stop for a moment. I have a free bonus set up for you. The problem is that we forget 90% of everything that we read after 7 days. Crazy fact, right? Here's the solution: we've created a printable, 1-page pdf summary for this book that you're reading now. All you have to do to get your free pdf summary is to go to the following website: **https://livetolearn.lpages.co/silviahill/**
Once you do, it will be intuitive. Enjoy, and thank you!

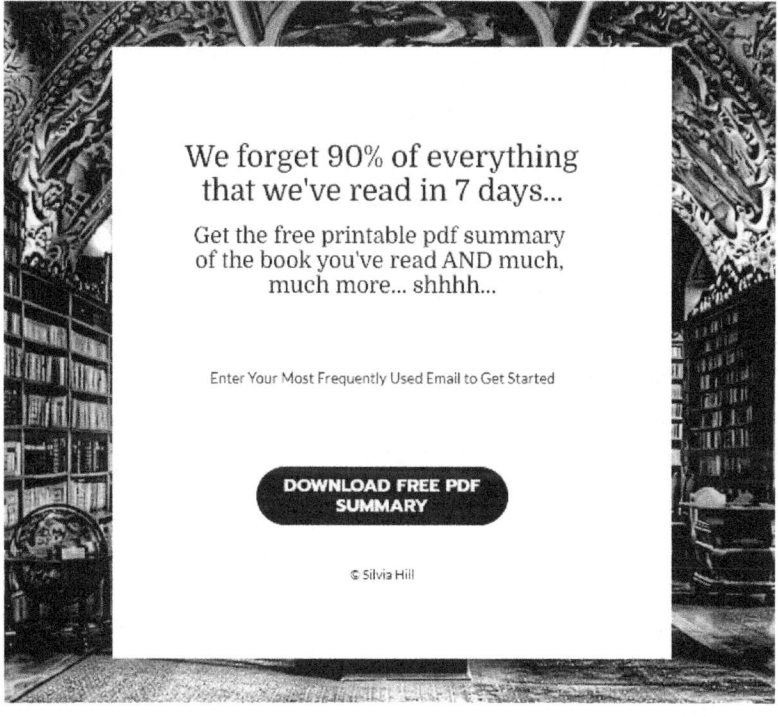

Contents

INTRODUCTION 1
CHAPTER 1: WHAT IS NUMEROLOGY? 3
    The Origin of Numerology 5
    Misconceptions about Numerology 8
CHAPTER 2: TYPES OF NUMEROLOGIES 13
    Chaldean Numerology 14
    Kabbalah Numerology: The Origins 16
    Tamil Numerology 21
    Chinese Numerology 23
    Western or Pythagorean Numerology 27
CHAPTER 3: SEEING SINGLE DIGITS? 30
    One: The Proactive and Primal Force 30
    Two: The Wise Diplomat 32
    Three: The Creative Spark 33
    Four: The Practical 35
    Five: The Dynamo 36
    Six: The Caregiver 37
    Seven: The Seeker 38
    Eight: The Wealthy 39
    Nine: The Renewer 40

CHAPTER 4: MASTER AND POWER NUMBERS 42
- 11 – The Master Visionary 43
- 22 – The Master Builder 45
- 33 – The Master Teacher 46
- Power Numbers 47
- 44 – The Master Healer 48
- 55 – The Unconventional Leader 49
- 66 – The Idealist 50
- 77 – The Master Helper 50
- 88 – The Master Entrepreneur 52
- 99 – The Master Humanitarian 52

CHAPTER 5: NUMEROLOGY AND ASTROLOGY 54
- The Link between Astrology and Numerology 55
- 1 – Ruled by the Sun (Zodiac Alter-Ego: Leo) 57
- 2 – Ruled by the Moon (Zodiac Alter-Ego: Cancer) 58
- 3 – Ruled by Jupiter (Zodiac Alter-Ego: Sagittarius, Pisces) ... 60
- 4 – Ruled by Uranus (Zodiac Alter-Ego: Aquarius) 61
- 5 – Ruled by Mercury (Zodiac Alter-Ego: Gemini, Virgo) 63
- 6 – Ruled by Venus (Zodiac Alter-Ego: Taurus, Libra) 65
- 7 – Ruled by Neptune (Zodiac Alter-Ego: Pisces) 66
- 8 – Ruled by Saturn (Zodiac Alter-Ego: Capricorn) 68
- 9 – Ruled by Mars (Zodiac Alter-Ego: Aries, Scorpio) 69

CHAPTER 6: THE KARMIC DEBT NUMBERS 71
- Karma in Numerology 72
- Signs You Have Karmic Debt 73
- What Numbers Carry Karmic Debt? 75
- Karmic Debt Number 13/4 76
- Karmic Debt Number 14/5 77
- Karmic Number 16/7 78
- Karmic Debt Number 19/1 80

CHAPTER 7: YOUR BIRTHDAY NUMBER 82
- Calculating Your Birthday Number 83

CHAPTER 8: LIFE PATH NUMBER 110
- Calculating Life Path Numbers 111

- Descriptions of Each Life Path Number 115

CHAPTER 9: YOUR GROWTH NUMBER 124
- What Are Growth Numbers? 124
- Calculating Growth Numbers 125
- Some Facts to Note about Growth Numbers 126
- 1 – Love, Light, Creator, Leader 127
- 2 – Diplomat, Harmony Bringer 127
- 3 – Creative, Vibrant, Expressive 128
- 4 – Reliable, Stable, Practical 128
- 5 – Ingenious, Adventurous, Optimistic 129
- 6 – Nurturing, Loving, Loyal 129
- 7 – Spiritual, Wise, Analytical 130
- 8 – Logical, Ambitious, Tenacious 130
- 9 – Mystic, Humanitarian, Teacher 131
- 11 – Goal-getter, Spiritual, Philanthropist 131
- 22 – Ambitious, Cooperative, Humanitarian 132
- 33 – Broad-minded, Selfless, Motivators/Guardians 132
- General Questions Concerning Growth and Name Number Calculators 133

CHAPTER 10: YOUR DESTINY NUMBER 135
- The Meaning and Importance of Destiny Numbers 135
- What Name to Use in Destiny Number Calculation 137
- Calculate Your Destiny Number 139
- The Meanings of Different Destiny Numbers 141

CHAPTER 11: THE SOUL URGE NUMBER 149
- How to Calculate the Soul Urge Number 150
- Soul Urge Number 1 153
- Soul Urge Number 2 154
- Soul Urge Number 3 155
- Soul Urge Number 4 156
- Soul Urge Number 5 157
- Soul Urge Number 6 158
- Soul Urge Number 7 158
- Soul Urge Number 8 159

SOUL URGE NUMBER 9 160
CHAPTER 12: YOUR PERSONALITY NUMBER **162**
   THE PERSONALITY NUMBER: WHAT DOES IT MEAN? 163
   CALCULATING YOUR PERSONALITY NUMBER 163
   PERSONALITY NUMBERS AND MEANINGS 165
CHAPTER 13: YOUR ATTITUDE NUMBER **170**
   HOW TO DETERMINE YOUR ATTITUDE NUMBER 171
   ATTITUDE NUMBER 1: YOU'RE DRIVEN 171
   ATTITUDE NUMBER 2: YOU'RE PERSEVERING 172
   ATTITUDE NUMBER 3: YOU'RE DYNAMIC 173
   ATTITUDE NUMBER 4: YOU'RE SENSITIVE 173
   ATTITUDE NUMBER 5: YOU'RE CREATIVE 174
   ATTITUDE NUMBER 6: THE ANALYST 175
   ATTITUDE NUMBER 7: YOU'RE HARMONIOUS 175
   ATTITUDE NUMBER 8: YOU'RE SECRETIVE 176
   ATTITUDE NUMBER 9: PRUDENCE PERSONIFIED 177
CHAPTER 14: YOUR HEREDITY NUMBER **178**
   HOW TO CALCULATE YOUR HEREDITARY NUMBER 179
   HEREDITARY NUMBER 1 180
   HEREDITARY NUMBER 2 180
   HEREDITARY NUMBER 3 181
   HEREDITARY NUMBER 4 182
   HEREDITARY NUMBER 5 183
   HEREDITARY NUMBER 6 184
   HEREDITARY NUMBER 7 184
   HEREDITARY NUMBER 8 185
   HEREDITARY NUMBER 9 186
CHAPTER 15: NUMEROLOGY AND COMPATIBILITY **188**
   COMPATIBILITY THROUGH THE LENS OF NUMEROLOGY 189
   COMBOS AND COMPATIBILITY 190
CHAPTER 16: ADD NUMEROLOGY TO YOUR DAILY LIFE **209**
   NUMEROLOGY FOR HIRING DECISIONS 210
   MAKING GOOD INVESTMENT DECISIONS 211

HERE'S ANOTHER BOOK BY SILVIA HILL THAT YOU MIGHT LIKE 218
FREE LIMITED TIME BONUS 219
INDEX OF TERMS 220
REFERENCES 222

Introduction

A Latin saying goes, *"omnis in numeris sita sunt."* What it means is that everything is hidden in numbers. This is further bolstered by the words of Madame Helena Petrovna Blavatsky, the most famous occult medium of the 19th century, who said, *"Number underlies form and guides sound."* It lies at the root of the manifested universe. This shows how powerful numbers are.

There is nothing in existence that does not possess shape, size, or dimension, all rooted in numbers. For this reason, numbers possess personal energy signatures or vibrations. Sound, for instance, is produced by vibrations that are audible at the rate of 20 to 20,000 vibrations per second. Above this benchmark is ultrasonic sound, and below it is subsonic.

Light, heat, speed, music, and friction are all dependent on vibration, hence numbers. Even color is composed of vibrations in a different octave. All the colors we see correspond to the wavelength of oscillation reflected. This is why, beyond the vibration of the color violet, the human eye cannot pick up additional colors; the vibration rate beyond violet is so minute that the human eye cannot capture it.

In this book, you'll learn the importance of numbers and begin to understand how they shape every aspect of your life. Unlike other books out there, this book is easy to understand, takes you by the hand, and shows you everything you need to know. You're about to have a much richer, fuller, more rewarding life than you ever thought possible, and you're going to do it using numbers. If you've never really liked numbers or if you hate math, your relationship with these powerful figures is about to do a 180-degree turn so fast it will make your head spin! Life is a numbers game, you see, and once you master it, it's like having all the cheat codes - you may feel invincible. So, if you're ready to begin, let's explore the wonderful world of numerology.

Chapter 1: What Is Numerology?

Humans have had an ambivalent relationship with numbers since time immemorial. Scratch marks on bones and cave walls from 30,000 years ago have been found to represent the lunar phase, which helped in the fields of agriculture and weather prediction. Ancient Babylonians used numbers to foretell eclipses and other phenomena.

Ancient Egyptian priests and priestesses – called hem netjer and hemet netjer – used numbers to foretell the flooding of the Nile. They did this using a nilometer, a vertical column submerged into the river that bears marks or intervals that indicate the river's depth. One of the historically important nilometers is on the elephantine island of Aswan, on the south border of Egypt.

Arithmancy, or arithomancy, originates from the Greek words *"arithmos"* (number) and *"manteia"* (divination), making it a science that studies divination using numbers. It was practiced by Hebrews, Chaldeans, and ancient Greeks – and has been succeeded by numerology today.

Despite their differences of opinion on certain subjects, Numerologists all agree that numbers have a mystical significance. In arithmancy and other forms of number mysticism, alphabets are assigned numbers using a set of rules. Words can be converted to numbers when their individual letters are added together. For this reason, people's names bear a specific significance. They also believe that everything in the world contains vibrations that can be traced back to the mystical properties of numbers. New age or modern numerologists incorporate powerful items like crystals, essential oils, gemstones, colors, and energy points (chakras) into their practice.

Disease has a specific vibration. This was proven by Dr. Abrams, an American physician who invented an instrument that measured the human body's reactions to determine the numerical value to be assigned to each disease. According to Abram, once numerical values are assigned to a disease or condition, their respective cures can be determined using numbers. Later, in 1985, Karin Lee Abraham published a book called "Healing through Numerology" in which she stated that every ailment had a specific vibrational rate. She constructed an illness chart and provided the best medication for the sick using her knowledge of numbers and vibrational frequencies.

As the theory stated, each number has an inherent unique vibration that gives it its specific characteristics. These characteristics may explain a person's behavior or determine the level of compatibility between two lovers. Numerology can help determine the lucky day or number of a person. Recurring numbers may give pointers that outline how the world works or the importance of certain events or people. To the average numerologist, nothing happens by chance. It is all predestined, and the answers lie in numbers.

The Origin of Numerology

The roots of numerology are incomplete without the Hebrew alphabet, the esoteric teachings of the Kabbalah, ancient teachings, and Pythagoras. This is because numerology is a science intricately woven with philosophies, myths, and mysticism.

Pythagoras is fondly called the "Father" of numbers. He was a Greek philosopher born in the year 569 B.C. At the age of 56, in the year 536 BC, he journeyed south of Italy, and in the Greek-speaking region called Crotona, he established the first university in history. There, he taught a combination of science and religion. Along with esoteric teachings, he taught the secrets of numbers and their vibrations to a select few. These discourses were so secret that they were never recorded in writing. Those who did so, intentionally or unintentionally, suffered the death penalty.

Many of his original works were lost after his death. Those who wrote about him did so hundreds of years after his demise. Writers who divulged the teachings later did so carefully by infusing lessons with a barrage of confusing information that would cause the attention of all but the true seeker to stray. Many historians have reason to believe that many of the discoveries and personality traits ascribed to him were the work of his devotees.

That notwithstanding, there are still a few manuscripts that have been preserved. Information about the university states that students abided by very stringent rules. They never had any in-person contact with Pythagoras until they had passed several initiations and were at a higher level of study. Even when contact was initiated, Pythagoras wore a robe that shielded him from prying eyes, so no one was really able to get an accurate description of him.

The father of numbers readily accepted children or initiates with a life path number of 7 into the school because, according to him, they were meant to learn the secret teachings. Other interested candidates who had a different path number had to pass a series of tests, such as being given a symbol like a triangle to meditate on.

Pythagoras opined that numbers lay at the heart of all creation. He claimed that understanding divinity could be achieved by understanding numbers. Suffice it to say that Pythagoras's science of numbers was founded on Kabbalistic teachings.

According to Underwood Dudley in his book "Numerology: or what Pythagoras wrought," the philosopher and his disciples were of the strong opinion that *"all is number."* Their study of number mysticism discovered that adding up a series of odd numbers starting with the number one always resulted in a square number.

This further enforced their principle that everything in the world can be described and measured in terms of proportions, dimensions, and numbers. In the same way, everything in this world, animate or inanimate, can be reduced to a number or set of numbers. This is a belief held by both scientists and mathematicians alike.

Modern numerologists ascribe intangible qualities to numbers and to individuals using their names. This may seem strange, but it is believed that the numbers one through to nine have special properties resulting from their inherent vibrational frequencies. Some of these qualities come from Pythagorean teachings. In contrast, others may result from how different cultures worldwide perceive and use numbers.

Numerologists typically use the name written on the birth certificate for a reading. According to them, unborn babies choose their names themselves and psychically communicate them to their parents to ensure they suit them and yield the correct numbers. The birth name holds more power over any nicknames, changed names, or names adopted post-matrimony.

To determine a person's number, the numerologist singles out each letter of their name and their corresponding numbers on a chart. The numbers are added together, and if the result is a two-digit number, both digits are added together to reveal a single digit, which becomes the personal number of that particular client.

Many practitioners enlist charts and diagrams to analyze numbers, letters in names, and their relationships with one another. The diagrams and charts are rooted in astrology and serve to add a deeper layer of information or meaning to the numerological reading. The charts used will be discussed later in the book. Regardless of the charts or methods employed to obtain a reading, the results sound similar to a horoscope.

You can use numerology to help you figure out the best career path suited to an individual's numerological makeup, lucky numbers, colors or days, positive behavioral attributes, negative tendencies. You can also learn a lot about their possible health issues (if birthdate is provided) and their desirable traits in a romantic partner.

Misconceptions about Numerology

Numerology is affected by the name change - Numerology is a science rooted in spirituality. Most people who understand what numerology is, describe it as applied mysticism. Therefore, it is wrong to see it as a simple numbers game that one can alter for personal gain.

If your name is changed at some point in your life, the numerologist will read both the birth name and the new name. However, the new name is a façade and will be treated as a subset of the original or given name.

Numbers attributed to the facade will not bear the same significance as the numbers attached to your original name and thus will be noted as a supplemental reading. Your free will and the decisions you make are the factors that can greatly influence your life and future. All numbers do is aid in self-interpretation so that your flaws are known, and you change your numerical vibration to influence public perception concerning you. Your fate and destiny are still yours to shape. Understanding this is the key to creating a truly balanced and fulfilled life.

When you have established a person's numbers, you can delve into their weaknesses, strengths, karmic debts, career, and relationship options, as well as help to gently align their thoughts and goals with reality, a form of manifestation if you will. This way, the individual is better equipped to face life's challenges with power and knowledge of what exists and which is to come.

Numerology readings are based on analyzing the numbers most significant in your life. They only provide an idea, a guide, or a precautionary measure concerning the past, present, and future. They are not designed to operate magically overnight, and neither do they guarantee a lack of well-being. No number completely answers life's questions or accurately predicts the future because reality, as we know it, is always changing.

Numerology is time-based - this is false. This is where numerology differs from astrology. In numerology, the exact time of birth or place of birth is not required for a reading, whereas in astrology, the birthplace and time of birth are pertinent pieces of information, without which readings cannot be conducted.

Numerology can help ascertain the perfect romantic partner - If this were true, wouldn't we all value our birth charts above our passports or social security numbers? Yes, it is possible to determine your personal number from a reading. This number may reveal certain aspects of your life (hidden or not), including what to expect in the perfect partner. Potential partners also have personal numbers. Hence, compatibility can be determined if a seasoned numerologist looks at both numbers.

After this, predictions will be offered concerning your future as a couple and whether the relationship is worth pursuing. Numerology has its gains, but is it something you should believe blindly over the free will exercised in choosing a mate? Should your choice of a partner depend first and foremost on matching numbers and gaining a favorable prediction?

Success is guaranteed with a name change - A true numerologist will never deceive you into believing that changing your name will guarantee a change of fortune, destiny, or fate. A new name changes your number vibrations so that people perceive you differently. It may also guide you toward seeing a better path, one that helps you achieve your goals and attract abundance.

Numerology readings are only associated with determining and reading the birth number - This assertion is one of the funniest and probably the most annoying to many practitioners. It's like saying milk is the only nutrition a cow can offer. (No offense intended to vegans and vegetarian readers.)

The belief that only birth numbers are of importance in a numerology reading is another false assertion and one that will be proven in future chapters of this book. Besides the "popular" birth number, many other numbers are significant during numerology readings. Personality numbers, life path numbers, balance numbers, karmic debt numbers, and others are numbers that can be interpreted in a typical numerology reading.

The myth of a lucky number or numbers - Not to rain on your parade, but a number, an object, or a person is lucky because of their belief and nothing else. All numbers are special, with unique vibrations and meanings.

According to numerology myths, the lucky numbers are 5, 6, and 8. People with the number 5 have earned their wealth through smart business dealings, strategic knowledge, wise investments, and hard work. Those with the number 6 gained wealth through marriage or inheritance, while those with the number 8 earned wealth through sheer luck. This is not always the case; anyone can lose money or gain money without necessarily having a lucky number in their corner.

If you are convinced that numerology will help you at the gambling tables or help you win the lottery, you should probably seek better financial advice, unless you enjoy having a hut at the end of Queer Street (a British colloquialism meaning to be in financial instability or embarrassment). Think long and hard before tattooing the numbers 3, 5, 6, or 8 on your wrist just because rumors say they are a sure-fire way to boundless wealth.

Numerology gives a certain level of significance to destiny numbers as they set the bar for your dreams and aspirations. Since numerology is not always an exact science and your life is not a 10th-grade chemistry project or a melt and pour soap masterclass, it is always advisable to refrain from giving too much relevance to destiny numbers (or numbers at all) over the trajectory of your life. The numbers are a guide. Deciding whether they directly affect your future is another kettle of fish entirely.

Karmic debt numbers are a bad omen - The obsession people have with these numbers always leads to misconceptions. Karmic numbers DO NOT represent the punishment or nemesis one will experience in this reality. Instead, they point toward behavioral patterns that should be avoided, such as abuse of power, abuse of freedom, or the presence of ego and negativity in previous lifetimes.

The concept of false firsts - In the hope of a stronger bond, most couples choose an auspicious marriage date to gain good fortune, have a longer-lasting marriage, and so on. They fail to realize that the day they met is more important in numerology than the date they pick to get married.

Only a small number of individuals are old souls - A famous delusion in numerology is the old soul myth, which is linked to only individuals with master numbers such as 11, 22, 33, etc. There are single-digit numbers such as 7 and 9, which are lonely spiritual numbers, and individuals with these numbers are seen as old souls as well.

Also, karmically challenged digits like 2 and 4 are additions of the master numbers 11 and 22. People with the number 2 are old souls existing to iron out past life connections, while the number 4 is an old soul balancing karmic debt in this life by suffering through health challenges.

A full chart must be created to understand your full numerological impression. This simply means an expert in numbers must interpret all of your numbers, including destiny, karmic debt, and expression numbers, to paint a full picture of your personality. When creating or referring to your numerology chart, you must understand that the numbers describe more than they predict, so it is wise not to limit yourself to whatever is told to you during a reading.

Numerology, as we have mentioned before, is a guide. It provides you with the incentive needed to make a decision at a time when you are confused about what step to take. Since numerology points out your strengths and weaknesses, you can make better-informed decisions and avoid pitfalls or situations that highlight your weaknesses or leave you feeling incompetent. Of course, there is always the option to convert your known weaknesses into strengths.

It is also superstitious to believe that you can be limited by numbers. For example, just because your life path number is 4 (which is usually an ominous number for most people) does not ultimately brand you as an unlucky person or indicate that fulfillment, fame, and love will elude you. It may help if you get several readings to obtain a clearer idea of your potential and limitations in life. Once you get rid of the misconceptions concerning numerology, the following chapters explain a few ways they can benefit you in your everyday life.

Chapter 2: Types of Numerologies

In earlier times, mathematics played a key role in the inception of numerology. Thousands of years ago, the practice of numbers was understood in a myriad of ways depending on the predominant culture, belief, and period during which it prevailed. True, it may not have gained scientific approval, but it did have a major effect on civilization in general.

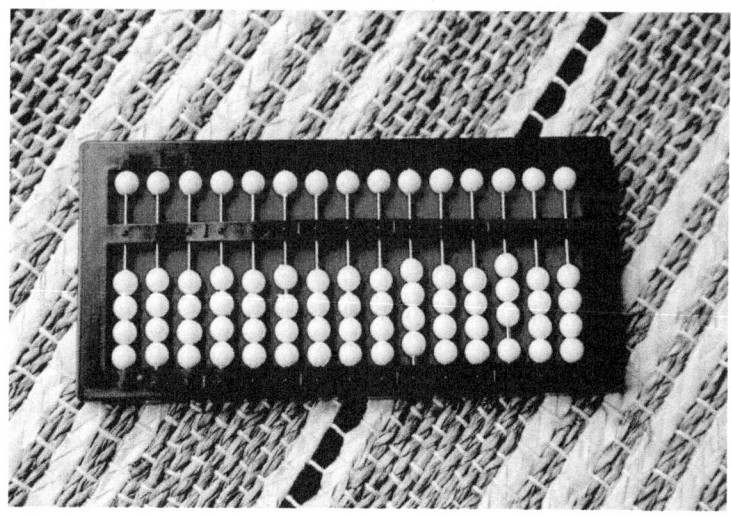

Every type of numerology in existence has its own unique way of interpreting numbers and analyzing results. Clear-cut and distinct information is obtained no matter which system is used, which, in turn, guides a person in gaining knowledge of themselves. There are five main typ-es of numerology, namely:

- Chaldean
- Kabbalah
- Tamil or Vedic
- Chinese
- Western or Pythagoras

Chaldean Numerology

Chaldean, or mystical, numerology is one of the most ancient numerology systems in the world. It originated from the Chaldeans, who walked the Earth in the 10th century BCE and briefly reigned over ancient Babylon (modern-day Iraq). The Chaldeans were famed for their superior intelligence and analytical skills. Besides numerology, they also contributed greatly to astrology and mathematics. They were also ardent students of the stars and planetary alignments - born scholars who sought to understand the mystical secrets of the universe.

Chaldean numerology is said to be the foundation of numerology, but historical records have shown the Vedic system existed a long time before the Chaldean system. Although this system is complex to master compared to others, it is the most accurate yet least popular method in use today.

This system is deeply rooted in the calculations of vibrations emitted by numbers, which lend them special or mystical characteristics. The vibrations of the numbers were said to have been written on ancient tablets by the gods dating back 2,500 years ago. Numbers go from one through to eight and are interpreted to yield meanings represented by various numbers (mostly one through to fifty-two). The number nine is considered sacred and is thus avoided during readings. In Chaldean numerology, the numbers assigned to each letter are not established by virtue of alphabetical order but by the innate vibrations possessed by each of the letters.

In other numerology methods, the approximated or reduced single digit is analyzed to study information about a person. If the sum arrived at is a nine, the value is retained. The Chaldean system uses both single and double-digit numbers, which are evaluated to yield calculations of vibrations and sounds. While the single digits describe the outer influences, the double digits offer information about the inner personality profile of the individual.

This way, it shows a complete and clear schematic of your life, including your likes, desires, dislikes, personality, and your path in life. Chaldean numerology is so precise that it even tracks energy fluctuations that surround you when another person calls your name. This is possible because calling out a name sends energy waves and frequencies to you and to those around you at that time.

Pandit Sethuraman is a famous Indian numerologist who did extensive research on both the Chaldean and Kabbalah numerology systems. He concluded that the ancient Chaldean system was the most authentic and precise system in existence. In Chaldean numerology, the name analyzed isn't your birth name but the name you are commonly known by. Hence, if your name is Katherine Herman, but you are commonly called Katie Herman, the Chaldean school of numerology will analyze the latter name instead of the former. Here are the numerical values for the letters of the alphabet in Chaldean numerology:

- A, I, J, Q, and Y have a value of 1
- B, K, and R have a value of 2
- C, G, L, and S have a value of 3

- D, M, T, have a value of 4
- E, H, N, and X have a value of 5
- U, V, and W have a value of 6
- O, and Z has a value of 7
- F and P have a value of 8

Kabbalah Numerology: The Origins

The Kabbalah doctrine is one with ancient origins in mystic Judaism. The Kabbalah is a primordial method used in divination and finding esoteric interpretations in Judaism and religious texts. *Kabbalah* itself translates to "tradition" in Hebrew and reflects on esoteric knowledge and principles that foster communion and a relationship between humans and the divine. Kabbalah places greater emphasis on human nature rather than on the body and everything else. The Kabbalistic practitioners of the early 10th century developed their own method of arcane interpretations of old Jewish texts. Today, this belief system serves as a reference through which followers of Judaism decipher deeper meanings in the Tanakh (Jewish Scripture).

Gematria: The Door to Kabbalistic Numerology

Gematria is the key numerological system showing the correspondence of Hebrew letters with numbers. It is the backbone of Kabbalah, and its correlation with Kabbalah forms the unique system that is Kabbalah numerology. The first Kabbalists created the Gematria to help understand and transcribe ancient Jewish texts. In the Gematria, every Hebrew script letter is given a specific number, right down to the final letter, which is assigned the number 900.

Understanding Kabbalah Numerology

The Kabbalah system of numbers is one of the more popular forms of numerology. It has received recognition and praise from celebrities like Britney Spears, Ashton Kutcher, Demi Moore, and Madonna. Its popularity steadily increases as more and more celebrities delve into Jewish esoteric wisdom, judging by the red strings on their wrists.

The significance of using your name to find your number can be attributed to the belief that names hold great significance when it comes to an individual's soul, destiny, and existence. The idea behind this system is the belief that one can gain a greater understanding of themselves from their personal numbers. It differs from other numerology systems in that it uses the individual's full name and not a significant number or a birth date.

In this system, names are given greater prominence than numbers. The script used originated from the Hebrew alphabet and is further analyzed by taking note of the birth name, which is useful in predictions. This should not be confused with a newer form of Kabbalah numerology that adapts Roman letters.

There are ten main energies used in Kabbalah for calculations and predictions. They are:

- Malkut "Sovereignty"
- Yesod "Foundation"

- Hod "Majesty"
- Netzach "Victory"
- Tiferet "Glory"
- Gevurah "Strength"
- Chesed "Mercy"
- Binah "Understanding"
- Chokhmah "Wisdom"
- Keter "Crown"

These energies contain 22 vibrations in a range of 1–400. Significance is placed on the wisdom derived from the soul and mind rather than that from flesh and blood. This is because the mind lacks physical existence while the flesh is material. Pure enlightenment requires a level of understanding beyond corporeal limitations in order to truly know oneself. In this system, each letter is assigned a specific value which is used for calculations and analyses.

Kabbalah numerology aims to foster honesty and a deeper understanding based on your number. This is because each name corresponds to a number, and the numbers are significant to you as a person and others who bear the same name or have the same number as you do.

Finding Your Kabbalah Number

The Kabbalah system, as mentioned above, is based on the Hebrew script, in which every letter corresponds with a particular number. The Kabbalah system may have its roots in the Hebrew alphabet, but the correlation of letters with numbers differs. These are the numerical values of the alphabet according to Kabbalah numerology:

- Letters A to I are numbered from 1 to 9, respectively.
- Letters J to R are also numbered 1 to 9, respectively.

- Letters S to Z are numbered 1 to 8, respectively.

Finding your Kabbalah number works by taking the numerical value of each letter in your given name; first name, middle name (where applicable), and surname, then adding them up to give a total value. If the total value is a double-digit or triple-digit number, simply add all the values to give a single-digit figure. It is common to see triple-digit figures in names with letters of high numerical value. After the summation, divide the figure by 9. If there is a remainder after the division, add one to the remainder to get your Kabbalah number.

For instance, if the sum of the letters in your name is 27, divide 27 by 9 to get 3, then add 1, and your Kabbalah number is given as 4. There are some cases where the sum may yield a number like 81. In this case, since it's a double-digit number, add 8 + 1 to give 9. Then as the rules go, divide the sum by 9, the resulting figure is 1, add 1, and the Kabbalah number becomes 2. Finding your Kabbalah number is pretty easy as long as the formula is followed.

The Significance Behind the Numbers in Kabbalah System

Like in all other systems, each number has an energy or vibration associated with it. The significance behind the numbers from 1 through to 9 is shown below.

1. Emergence and progress.

2. Balance, care, and expansion.

3. Love, innovation, optimism, and originality.

4. Misfortune, adversity, and practicality.

5. Change, formation, creation, free spirit.

6. Accomplishment, fulfillment, result, nurturing.

7. Spirituality and enlightenment.

8. Inspiration, abundance, impulse, and success.

9. Serendipity, luck, selflessness, and accomplishment.

Each number has multiple meanings and energetic signatures, so just because your number is the ominous 4 and not as serendipitous as the numbers 2 or 9, there is no need to worry. The numbers are only a guide and not a prediction of a lack of success or happiness in your walk through life. The numbers merely warn you of the challenges ahead. But who in life does not have challenges? They are inevitable for even those assigned the luckier Kabbalah numbers. Kabbalah numbers intend to advise you on the best course of action to take regardless of whatever bumps in the road lie ahead.

What Makes Kabbalah Numerology Special?

What makes the Kabbalah system unique is the fact that it bridges the gap between the finite and infinite, the physical and metaphysical realms, helping us understand the connection between the finite and material world and the infinite Godhead, or Ein Sol. The key difference between the Chaldean and Kabbalah systems of numerology is the respective values of certain letters which differ between these systems.

The letter "A" has the value of 1 in both methods, whereas the letter "V" has the value of 6 in Chaldean numerology while it corresponds to the number 4 in Kabbalah. This is the case because the range of numbers in the Kabbalah system is greater than in other systems—approximately 400 life paths that accrue to 22 letters or vibrations.

Secondly, other Western and Chaldean numerology methods will evaluate birth dates and assign a number known as the life path number based on them. The Kabbalah only analyzes the given name as it appears on the birth certificate. For this reason, practitioners believe this system to be less accurate when compared to other numerology methods.

Tamil Numerology

Tamil numerology is also called Vedic or South Indian numerology. It is named after Tamil Nadu, a state in south India. In the past, it was studied by Indian sages and is one of the oldest forms of numerology still in existence. Like in the Kabbalah system, the numbers range from one through to nine. Each number possesses a specific vibration or characteristic that increases self-awareness and knowledge.

This system posits that every soul chooses to reveal themselves using a birthday and a vibration that allows for further evolution of their consciousness on this plane. The numbers ascribed to each individual stand for their ego, psychological wellbeing, and the karmic remnants they possess throughout their lifetime. This helps to identify strengths and weaknesses they were born with so they can learn from their experience in this lifetime. This numerology method makes use of Vedic squares, a variant of the 9 by 9 multiplication table found in traditional Islamic art, motifs, and Hindu geometrical configurations.

The Vedic tables in Tamil numerology show the spiritual link between an event and a number that helps in its prediction. The tables can also be used to analyze the vibrational qualities of baby names, comprehend the harmonic patterns and alignments of planets in astrology, foretell the future to a great extent, and discover personality traits. On the other hand, name-number calculation can be a bit taxing since it requires complex measurements depending on the sound frequency produced by each number.

In Tamil numerology, three numbers are associated with every individual: The *destiny number, the psychic number*, and the *name number.* The psychic number is determined by the individual's birth date. For instance, if the birth date is March 20th, the psychic number will be 2+0=2. The psychic number is 2. The psychic number gives an idea of the individual's perception of themselves, their core beliefs, and the personality attributes they exhibit. It hints at how the individual treats or deals with those around them and gives insight into their karma or their actions in a past life.

The destiny number tells how the world sees you and is calculated by adding the numbers in your birth date together. Destiny numbers signify how the world perceives you. This is calculated by summing up the numbers in your birth date and birth year to a single digit. So, on March 20th, 2015, it would be 3+2+0+2+0+1+5=13 and, furthermore, 1+3=4. Hence, the person would have a destiny number of 4.

The name number tells us of the individual's relationship with others. It is calculated using a mathematical formula based on the sound frequencies that accrue to a certain number.

For instance, in Tamil numerology, the number 4, which is deemed unlucky in the Kabbalah system, is ruled by Uranus. Individuals who are pragmatic, humble, practical, and bubbly are number four. They are adventure seekers who are quite invested in life's physical and material aspects. They are also famous for being reliable, trustworthy, and great confidants. Their practicality and discipline make them suitable for managerial and organizational positions. In fact, the best jobs for number four individuals involve finance and taxes.

On the other hand, numbers representing accomplishment and success in Kabbalah numerology actually indicate failure with money in Tamil numerology due to their overly generous nature and need for worldly comforts. How ironic is that?

Tamil Letter-Number Correspondence

Planet	Number	Alphabet
Sun	1	A, I, J, Q, Y
Moon	2	B, K, R
Jupiter	3	C, G, L, S
Rahu/Uranus	4	D, M, T
Mercury	5	E, H, N, X
Venus	6	U, V, W
Ketu/Neptune	7	O, Z
Saturn	8	P, F
Mars	9	-

Chinese Numerology

The Chinese system of numerology has been in use for over 4,000 years. It is founded on mysticism and the ancient knowledge of the I-Ching. The popular assumption behind this system is that numbers could be auspicious or inauspicious based on the Chinese word that the number is homophonous with or similar to in pronunciation.

The practice of assigning good or bad luck to numbers is not unique to the Chinese. Other East Asian nations with a history of similar beliefs and Han characters adopt this practice. This is because luck in East Asian culture is related to the concept of destiny, so if someone is deemed lucky, their destiny is believed to have been blessed by the gods. For instance, the Chinese word for "one" is homophonous with the Mandarin word for "honor." Here, one is neither lucky nor unlucky, but this may symbolize loneliness or single status. The number 8 is homophonous with the Mandarin word for prosperity and is termed an auspicious number. The number 9 signifies power/eternity, while the number 4 is similar in pronunciation to the Chinese word for death or misfortune. Hence, it is avoided by the Chinese.

Following this analogy, number combinations are valued for their reference to luck and prosperity, such as 28, 39, 26, etc. Along with their belief in fate and luck, the Chinese study mystical number combinations and associated relationships in nature. For instance, they believe that there are 12 vessels that circulate air and blood throughout the body. These vessels coincide with the 12 rivers flowing through the central kingdom. Also, the 365 days in the year are connected mystically to the 365 body parts used to locate acupuncture points in Chinese unorthodox medicine.

The simplest method of Chinese numerology is the Lo Shu Square. This square is based on the story of a tortoise that possessed nine perfect squares on its shell, as noted by the Emperor seated on the Luo River's banks.

The early Lo Shu square was called the magic square because it had three rows and columns of numbers, which added up to 15, regardless of whether the numbers were taken horizontally, vertically, or diagonally. Another peculiar feature of the square is that even numbers are arranged at the corners while the odd numbers form a cross or T-shape in the middle. The arrangement of numbers in the square looks something like this:

4	9	2
3	5	7
8	1	6

In recent times, the Chinese have developed a modern version of the magic square called the "hidden cross" to teach Chinese numerology to westerners. The hidden cross does not use the lunar year and has simpler arithmetic calculations. The numbers in the hidden cross are arranged thus:

3	6	9
2	5	8
1	4	7

Interpreting the outcomes of either the magic square or the hidden cross requires an in-depth knowledge of what the squares and the numbers symbolize. The top row in the square stands for mental capabilities, e.g., analytical ability; the bottom row signifies practical or the rational mind, strength, physical strength, or athleticism, while the middle row represents emotions, intuition, and feelings. According to the Chinese system, the number 1, for instance, is an indicator of interpersonal relationships. If, according to the readings, you have:

- **One 1:** This shows you have difficulty expressing your thoughts to others.

- **Two 1s:** You have an easy time communicating with and understanding others.

- **Three 1s:** You can communicate with others but are prone to occasional mood swings.

- **Four 1s:** Your caring and sensitive nature is admirable, but you find it hard to verbalize.

- **Five or More 1s:** You find social situations uncomfortable. You adopt unhealthy coping mechanisms such as over-drinking or overeating.

It is easy for skeptics to dismiss the beliefs of East Asians as superstitious and over the top, but their belief in the power of numbers permeates every aspect of their daily lives. In 1988, for instance, many pregnant Chinese women trooped to the hospital in droves to ask for a cesarean section to have their babies born as "dragon children" with double prosperity destinies. Chinese entrepreneurs also employ numerology when naming their businesses in the hope that this will attract good fortune and a large customer base.

The Chinese government often auctions cars with inauspicious license plates; individuals pay a pretty penny to have customized automobile license plates, up to $60,000 or higher! Also, in Chinese numerology, the numbers are linked to an element:

- Water – 1
- Earth – 2, 5, and 8
- Wood – 3 and 4
- Metal – 6 and 7
- Fire – 9

The Asians are not the only people who are superstitious about numbers. Many westerners, for instance, are afraid of the number 13, particularly when it falls on a Friday. Skeptics fathom the fear of 13, which stems from the fact that Judas Iscariot was the 13th person to arrive at the venue of the last supper. Although historians believe that the inauspicious 13 and the fear of it began much earlier, Airlines do not have a 13th row. Hotels omit 13th floors from their buildings. Formula 1 race cars are numbered 12, then 14, skipping the number 13. The fear of number 13 even has a name which is *triskaidekaphobia.*

In China, instead of the number 13, the number 4 is considered ominous because it has the same pronunciation as the Chinese word for death. In Japan, the ominous number is 9 because it has the same pronunciation as the Japanese term for suffering or torture. Italians are wary of the number 17 because, in roman numerals, it is interpreted as XVII, which could be rearranged to

VIXI, meaning "my life is over." I could go on and on about the love-hate relationship humans have with numbers, but that isn't the purpose of this book.

Western or Pythagorean Numerology

This form of numerology will be the main focus of this book. The Chaldean system had an immense influence on the ancient Greeks, and hence the Pythagorean system developed. It was during the era of Greek imperialism and when taking control of Babylon that the Greeks discovered the Chaldean numerology scripts, and from these, the western system was born.

Western or Pythagorean numerology is a system developed by the Greek philosopher and mathematician Pythagoras. He invented this system because he believed everything in nature could be reduced to numbers or mathematical calculations. This is a more modern system and that which this book will focus primarily on, although ideas will be imported from other forms of numerology.

Pythagoras believed that a lot could be learned about a person from their name and core number. He also proposed that every number had both a positive and negative quality.

Inspired by the Chaldean script, he formulated a logical method of numbers. His addition of mathematical knowledge and logic lent some credence to the system. The Pythagorean system has a linear progression in the affinity between letters and numbers. The numbers range from one to nine and hold specific vibrations like all other systems. He assigned the numbers 1 through to 9 in the following sequence: A = 1, B = 2, until I = 9.

There is also the existence of master numbers like 11, 22, and 33. These numbers are usually rounded to a single digit. The numbers allow one to draw a complete chart linked to the planets and astrology that describes all the attributes of the individual requesting a reading as well as maps out a clear-cut trajectory/pattern of life. This system is commonly used by western nations and is easily the most popular form of numerology out there.

The Pythagorean chart looks something like this:

1	2	3	4	5	6	7	8	9
A	B	C	D	E	F	G	H	I
J	K	L	M	N	O	P	Q	R
S	T	U	V	W	X	Y	Z	

The Spread of Pythagorean Numerology

After his death, Pythagorean numerology achieved fame and acceptance throughout the mathematical community, and several Greek philosophers and mathematicians adopted his theories. Plato, in particular, in his book called *Timaeus*, written in the 4th century B.C., borrows Pythagorean numerology in describing cosmology as a product of the divine ruled by numerical and mathematical truths.

Even today, western numerology is continuously evolving and has formed the foundations of major arcane societies such as Freemasons, Rosicrucians, and the Theosophical Society.

The person to credit for the spread of numerology in the past century is William John Warner (Count Louis Harmon to some people) or Cheiro. This Irish astrologer and master of the occult coined his moniker from the word "Cheiromancy"—the art of palm reading. Cheiro was a self-acclaimed clairvoyant who used his talent for numbers and the mystic sciences to predict events and conduct readings for popular figures such as Mark Twain, Thomas Edison, and the Prince of Wales.

Numbers in the Pythagorean System

Pythagorean numerology analyzes five main numbers:

1. Life path number
2. Birthday number
3. Personality number
4. Heart's desire number
5. Expression number

Each number reveals a different facet of an individual's persona. When combined, they give detailed insight into a person's character, the challenges they face, and the talents they might have. The numbers will be discussed in detail in later chapters.

Every numerology system is different. Each bears an identity and pattern of calculation unique to them. No system is better than the other, as different countries and people tend to favor systems closer to home. Each will give varying results based on belief and honesty. However, these days, the Pythagorean system of numbers has become more mainstream because modern practitioners laud it as the most accurate and easy-to-use system in existence.

With advancements in technology and the advent of the internet, many numerology calculations are done online. Popular numerology practitioners advertise their art and the form of numerology they practice, so you can choose what works best for you when faced with the different forms of numerology calculators on the internet.

Chapter 3: Seeing Single Digits?

The numbers one through to nine form the backbone of numerology since all multiple digits can be reduced to a single digit. For example, 25 can be reduced to 7, 18 to 9, and so on. For example, certain double-digit figures have unique meanings, such as 13, 14, 16, and 19, which are karmic debt numbers, and 11, 22, 33, and so on, which are master numbers. This chapter will cover the single digits 1 through to 9. You will learn how each number affects you, your health, career, love life, etc., and what it means for you if you see them repeatedly.

One: The Proactive and Primal Force

One is the number of creativity, efficiency, leadership, and autonomy. Seeing this number repeatedly could symbolize the start of something fresh and original in your life. The number 1 represents an individual who is creative and empowered to bring their desires into reality.

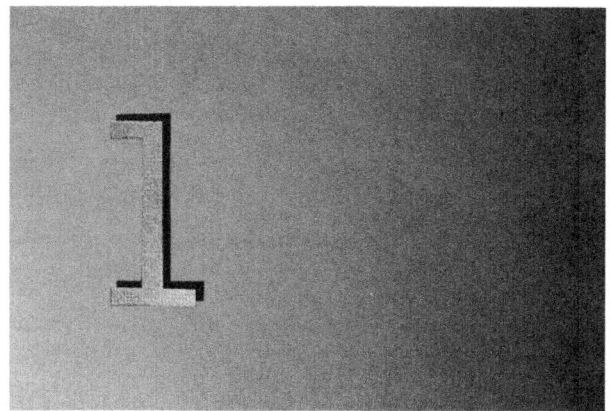

You are likely to come across this number many times on your spiritual journey. You may find that you usually have many questions before seeing the number 1. You could be searching for answers in your love life or career. The number 1 signifies that you are close to the breakthrough you have been waiting for. When this happens, be mindful of what you focus on since the positive focus is an integral part of the manifestation process.

In terms of love and your love life, people with life path number 1 are very demanding and emotionally difficult to handle. If you and someone with the number 1 are in a relationship, it signifies a deepening of the bond between you and your partner. If you are single, then you won't be single for long because someone amazing is about to come and sweep you off your feet - someone who will change the course of your life forever! Just listen to your heart and let it guide you to your intended destination.

Number 1 is a reminder to count your blessings. The divine wants to remind you of the fact that the highest expression of yourself is seen in the value and love you bring to the lives of others. It reiterates the love you have from family and friends. You have so much that you take for granted, and this number reminds you that it's these little things that make your life truly beautiful. Recognize the blessings you do have so that the universe sends more your way.

Two: The Wise Diplomat

The number 2 is the first prime number and is called the "odd" prime. It is a number that signifies balance, harmony, and partnership. On the flip side, it symbolizes conflict and resistance. In Asia, 2 is known as the number of good luck. A popular Chinese adage goes thus, *"Hao shi cheng shuang,"* which means good things come in pairs. It is quite common to see Asians carve a symbol in pairs on products, brand names, etc., to signify twice the value and twice the happiness. In the lunar year, the Chinese people exchange sweet oranges in multiples of two.

The vibrational signature of the number 2 is that of service, receptivity, and cooperation. Seeing the number 2 is a sign that the universe knows you are a hard worker and seeks to encourage you. However, you must be open to compromises and peaceful conflict resolutions, especially with people you loathe being around. The number 2 is also a sign that you will achieve the security and stability you deeply crave. The key is to stay alert and receptive both to your needs and that of others.

This number signifies that you ought to stop being pushy and allow the universe to work in your favor. It also reminds you that everyone you meet in your life is an avenue through which you can grow as a human being. In terms of progress and achievement, the number 2 symbolizes that you will soon be rewarded for your hard work and that the universe will rejoice with you in your achievements. All that is left for you to do is close that chapter of your life and remember the lessons you have gained from your experience since every step you take brings you closer to your divine mission.

In love and relationships, the number two is a symbol of fidelity and trust. These two virtues will come in handy in nurturing the present relationship you have with your partner. Communication and empathy are always key to a harmonious relationship. Your ego has no place here.

Three: The Creative Spark

Three is a number representative of the divine trinity, a symbol of the unity of mind, soul, and body. As such, it symbolizes guidance, protection, and support from the divine realm.

The number 3 in spirituality is considered the number of concordance and wisdom. It embodies the energy of joy, hope, advancement, creativity, communication, inner guidance, and materialization. The number 3 may appear in our experience at any time of day, either in work-related files, addresses, or phone numbers. You may also find yourself doing things in threes, going to a particular place, or getting the same item three times.

Constantly seeing the number 3 is a sign of good things to come. It also means you should have more faith in your abilities, be more self-assured, and remain positive in thought and deed. Seeing this number means you are in alignment with your spiritual guides and guardian angel. It reminds you to live life fully by doing the things you love. Learning that skill you have been putting off or engaging in the hobby you have always wanted to do may always seem daunting with number 3, but it is always in your best interest. Failure to tap into your creative well of energy or spontaneity will lead you to the brink of depression and anxiety.

In love, 3 urges you to be more confident, express yourself and listen to your heart. It may signify the right time to begin something new with a potential love interest if you are single. With the number 3, your intuition is strong, and you should learn to believe in yourself more.

In terms of social connection, 3 reminds you of how much you have relegated your social life to the back burner, even though you are an affable person. Your guardian angel is encouraging you to surround yourself with like-minded people who share your vision and passion. This way, they will fuel your energy and motivation.

This will, in turn, broaden your horizons and give you a better perspective regarding the next steps to take in life.

Four: The Practical

The number 4 is symbolic of the four winds in the cardinal points - north, east, west, and south - which are also the four sacred directions. Also, the main elements in existence are water, air, earth, and fire.

The number 4 is more concerned with earthly and practical matters. A number 4 persona is well organized, methodical, practical, and honest in their dealings. A born leader, the number four person is mature and balanced. However, some of their vices like impatience, obstinacy, and intolerance may creep in. The number 4 could also be a reminder to make your usually rigid mindset more flexible; only this way will you be on the right path to awakening the dormant talents you have embedded within.

Constantly seeing the number 4 is a message from the guardian angels telling you the steps needed to achieve your goals. They are advising diligence, organization, discipline, and dedication in all endeavors while they look out for you and work on your behalf.

This number also symbolizes additional motivation and determination you need to cross the finish line in whatever challenges you are facing at the moment. The process of transformation, though tough, will make you a better person. Open your heart and eyes to new possibilities and let positive energies flow inward.

In love, the number indicates a need to bring stability into your relationship to strengthen the bond between you and your partner.

Five: The Dynamo

From all indications, 5 symbolizes several important things, from good luck to future predictions and necromancy. To a lot of people, the number five represents good luck.

The number 5 indicates positive change, so seeing this number is a sign that more of them are about to flood your life, and everything will turn out to be in your favor. Number 5 is linked to individualism, independence, intelligence, curiosity, liberty, and adventure. Number 5 people, according to numerology, are known for always being on the move, never staying in a place, or sticking to one thing for too long.

5 tells you to slow down, be more responsible and consider the future as much as you enjoy living in the present. Since the number 5 is concerned with sensual experience (which is ever-changing), the universe urges you through this number to embrace the sphere of existence that remains constant throughout life—the spirit.

In terms of health, the number 5 indicates a necessity to make lifestyle changes to improve mental and physical health and vitality. You may be seeing this number because you have taken on some sensual habits that are detrimental to your health and spirit. It simply means you need to step back from the path you have taken and re-evaluate because you are not living up to your full potential. Learn from your life experiences and quit burying your head in the sand. It is time to take charge of your life and create your own destiny because nothing is a coincidence.

Six: The Caregiver

In esoteric teachings, 6 is represented by the hexagon, which, when dissected, is composed of two overlapping triangles, much like the number six is formed by the summation of two number threes. The hexagon is seen in the seal of Solomon and the Star of David. According to esoteric teachings, it connotes the integration of the conscious mind (as seen by the upward-facing triangle) and the unconscious mind (the downward-facing triangle). This union of two opposites—the conscious and unconscious mind—represents harmony and balance.

6 teaches us the importance of finding balance in our lives. A lot of times, humans are carried away by the goings-on in the external world. A 6 represents an obsession with things like academic qualifications, finances, careers, and fitness goals. The number 6 appears to remind you not to allow these outward achievements to overshadow your spiritual well-being.

When this number frequently appears in your life, it serves as a reminder to find a way to balance your emotions and time, as well as being careful in your career and domestic life. Refuse to burden yourself with more responsibilities than you can handle, despite your loving and giving nature.

The number 6 is also a wake-up call for you to discover your triggers or those things that make you emotionally restless or drawn to self-sabotage and destructive behaviors. Strive for contentment instead of material things.

The number 6 urges you to be more aware of the energy you transmute and take time to develop the hidden qualities in your subconscious. Allow repressed memories to surface and, dare I say it, be selfish. It is time for you to put yourself first for a change. Practice self-love while finding time in between to show love to others.

Seven: The Seeker

The number 7 is a blend of the diligent 4 and the mystical 3. As a result of this, 7 embodies the perfect blend of practical and metaphysical attributes. It is a number associated with spiritual awakening, inner wisdom, intuition, self-awareness, and mysticism.

7 has an extremely high frequency and vibration, so this is not the time to doubt your choices and decisions. Put less faith in the opinions of others and more faith in your own instincts because the universe is completely behind you.

7 is also known as a herald of good luck, happiness, and material wealth. When it appears before you constantly, it is a powerful embodiment of the patience, persistence, and inner will you possess. It is a reminder that you can do whatever you set your mind to, as long as you believe in your abilities.

In love, 7 may mean that you are not totally open to your significant other. Hiding or suppressing your emotions or refusing to discuss them to avoid conflict can negatively impact you and your relationship in the long run. Also, 7 cautions you when meeting new people.

Eight: The Wealthy

8 is a sign that abundance will soon be coming your way. 8 symbolizes the flow of energy and infinite perfection. In numerology, a person with a life path or birth number 8 is usually associated with success, enormous miracles, power, and abundance. 8 is the number of rewards, justice, and balancing the scales. For this reason, it is one of the karmic numbers in numerology.

As a karmic number, 8 apprises you of how you will get whatever you put out into the universe. Show kindness and love, and it will be returned to you tenfold. The opposite will also come back to you, so be careful of your actions and approach to life.

In esoteric teachings, 8 is the union of two squares (connoting earthly order) and the octagon, which represents the start of the transformation of the square into a circle (connoting eternal order).

Seeing this number constantly is a reminder to you to have more faith in yourself and step out of your comfort zone. 8 is linked to self-esteem, harmony, and confidence, so do not be afraid to trust your gut and take bold steps. The number 8 may indicate that you will manage to achieve balance in life after a long period of strife and discomfort. As a result of your hard work, prosperity and abundance are on the horizon for you. With the number 8, expect a financial boom in the near future.

In love, 8 points to your relationship problems being resolved. If you are single, it means that your search for true love may be over, and the partner you deserve will come into your life faster than you expected.

Nine: The Renewer

Numerologists and esoteric scholars regard 9 as the number of completion or culmination of a cycle after which numbers revert to zero, as seen in the Gematria. In esoteric teachings, 9 represents the last dimension where celestial energy manifests itself in the material world.

From a spiritual standpoint, the number nine represents intellect, influence, humanitarianism, compassion, enlightenment, and innovation. The goal of those on life path 9 is to understand the gifts they possess and teach them to others.

It signifies your guardian angel is trying to convey a message. Seeing 9 constantly might mean that someone you care about is in need of your assistance. So, find ways to help those around you with the little that you do have. Your ability to show empathy to others may be amplified at this time, so take measures to positively influence those around you. By doing this, you will reap the rewards of joy and happiness.

If you are thinking of pursuing a new career or changing jobs and you see the number 9, it represents a clarion call for you to consider a vocation that is more humanitarian – since it will be more fulfilling in the long run.

In love, 9 urges you to look inward and evaluate your path together with your significant other to see if you are both on the right path. It may mean it's time to spice things up in the bedroom to increase your bond.

Chapter 4: Master and Power Numbers

The master numbers consist of the numbers 11, 22, and 33. These numbers come with special traits and higher vibrations compared to single-digit numbers. On a karmic level, individuals with master numbers have learned all the lessons that accrue to the single digits 1–9 before their birth and are on this plane to improve humanity.

Having a master number as part of your core numbers could be a source of strength, but I won't pretend it does not pose its own set of challenges. Finding ways to cope and take control of the curveballs and downsides associated with master numbers is the best way to live a happy and prosperous life.

As 11, 22, and 33 comprise 1, 2, and 3, respectively, they are considered the **ONLY** master numbers because they possess elevated insight and form the triangle of the enlightenment - a triangle of revelation, manifestation, growth, and a higher perspective. In the triangle, 11 is the creator and visionary, 22 is the builder of visions who fine-tunes the dreams brought forth by 11, and 33 represents the creative who shares the finished vision with the rest of the world.

Having a master number does not guarantee success because the freedom of choice trumps all predictions. It is possible for you to have more than one master number in your chart. The potential and power are present, but since success won't drop in your lap, you will require focus, effort, and opportunity to showcase your talents to the world.

Master number guidance is only applied when discovered in your numerology chart as core numbers (derived from your birthday or life path number), soul urge numbers, destiny numbers, or personality numbers. Those numbers will be discussed in detail in further chapters. Also, Pythagorean numerology is the only system of numerology used in master number determination. Because of the power in these numbers, it is advised that you become familiar and in tune with all the numbers that appear on your chart to decipher whether master numbers are hidden within your chart.

11 — The Master Visionary

This number is made of double ones and symbolizes the height of both masculine energy (1) and feminine energy (2) derived when the master number is reduced to a single digit. For this reason, this master number combines the intuition and confidence of 1 with the sensitive intuition of the number 2. The expression of 11 may be confident intuition, but it constantly walks a tightrope between greatness and self-destruction. As the first of the master numbers, it has the spiritual quality of *"as above, so below."*

In many readings, 11 is reduced to 2, but where 2 is a passive and quiet follower, 11 is fiercely independent, a loner, and a leader. Having double the qualities of the artistically inspiring and spiritual number 1, number 11 is called the psychic master since such persons are interested in exploring beyond the barriers of the non-physical dimension while combining it with empathy, sensitivity, and intuition.

An 11 individual is spiritual, cooperative, and sensitive. This enables them to sense subtle auras and energies – and possess a *psychic knowing*. It's almost like they can hear your thoughts out loud and sense your fears. This strong sense of awareness is, to them, both a blessing and a curse. The high-spirited 11 places more emphasis on belief, faith, and credence. They rely more on their inner spiritual voice instead of their logical brain. Hence, they are not the most rational thinkers in the group.

Those with this number are regarded as old souls, able to handle stressful situations in a calm and diplomatic manner. 11 is a number linked to faith and the future. As such, individuals with this number may have some qualities of clairvoyance, prophecy, or other psychic abilities. The downside for people having this number is that when their energies are not focused on a particular endeavor, they tend to be restless, fearful, and even anxious. This may lead to panic attacks and the development of phobias. They also suffer from vulnerability to stress, impracticality, self-conflict, and a lack of self-confidence.

The number 11 reminds you of the limitless opportunities that await exploration. Do not be afraid to act on anything that gives you a sense of joy and purpose. Embrace new beginnings and make small changes to the circle of people you surround yourself with.

22 — The Master Builder

This is one of the most successful of the master numbers. 22 is brimming with energy and potential, which is why such individuals must work to achieve success in causes larger than themselves. They are born to serve humanity as a whole. Positive traits associated with this number include practicality, discipline, ambition, idealism, great accomplishments, self-confidence, and dynamism. Negative traits include arrogance, aloofness, aimlessness, and a propensity to micromanage and manipulate others.

22 has a lot of esoteric significance. The original Hebrew alphabet consists of 22 letters, symbolic of everything from creation to eternity.

This master number has all the inspirational qualities of 11 and the down-to-earth nature of 4. As long as these individuals work towards humanitarian causes instead of personal ambition, they have the capacity to make every dream of theirs come true. This actualization of dreams is a trait of 4, which 22 is reduced to. If you have a life path of 22, you will find that you are able to unite many to achieve a single goal. You are a visionary who possesses not only the ability to see potential in a certain idea, but also one who can bring that idea to life. Somehow, you already know what will work and what won't. This is probably the reason why you are geared towards controlling or manipulating others instead of surrendering your will to the greater cause.

If your energies are not devoted to practical affairs, you will lose your ambition and potential. This leads to you being as tightly wound as an analog clock in your youth. The trick here is to have enough work to avoid being idle and balance work with a conduit to expel negative energy, for instance, comedy or a hobby. In love, you find it difficult to face your shortcomings. Your intense focus on your goals could lead to mood swings and frigidity, which affect your love life.

33 — The Master Teacher

This is the most spiritually evolved and enlightened of the master numbers. 33 possesses a higher vibration than 6. What makes this master number special is its extremely sincere devotion. It is the most influential of the three master numbers since it has the attributes of both 11 and 22. They are simply expressed to a greater degree.

A fully evolved 33 is extremely rare. It has a blend of the powers of creativity and expression (3) and the caregiver/teacher extraordinaire vibe (6). It is no surprise that it is the rarest among the master numbers. Even if you have a 66 in your core number, mastering the traits that go with it is not for the faint of heart.

Numerous instances exist that speak to the divine status of the number 33. The human spine, for instance, has 33 segments. The tree of life in the Jewish Kabbalah has 22 paths, 10 globes, and an invisible death, making it a total of 33 steps to enlightenment. The first temple of Solomon stood for 33 years. Jesus lived 33 years, and King David reigned for 33 years.

Seeing this number constantly is a sign from the angels that you need to quit being a wallflower and express your opinions more. It is a number that usually appears to those feeling lost and forlorn. Hence, it is an assurance that a series of events that will cause personal growth are incoming. However, you need to meditate on your past actions so that you can become a better version of yourself. Forgive yourself for your past and be grateful for how far you have come and how strong you have become.

In love and relationships, 33 is a sign for you to rid yourself of toxic friendships and people and focus your energy on those who love you the way you deserve to be loved. Stop thinking about what used to be or what once was and shift your mental energy to what is and what is to come.

Power Numbers

These are also called "goal," "reality, "maturity, or "realization" numbers. Like master numbers, power numbers are double digits with identical numbers, making them possess double the traits of their component numbers. Power numbers are derived by summing up the destiny numbers and the life path number. Think of master and power numbers as twins with similar attributes working together. Their potential for success is greatly amplified.

Your power numbers contain the energy available to accomplish your life goals and enhance your chosen career. It is an indication of how you can make a difference in the world and the lives of those around you on your path toward finding happiness in life. The power numbers are 44, 55, 66, 77, 88, and 99.

The impact of power energy does not come into full force immediately after awakening. It takes a few years. Around middle age (40-45), its resonance becomes clearer, and your perspective on the world shifts. How dramatic this shift is will depend on whether you have a power number with single dissimilar digits or double yet similar digits. If the former is the case, your power number obtains a new resonance. In the case of the latter, the resonance is amplified.

Here, we will calculate the power number of the famous South African entrepreneur, Elon Reeve Musk, using the Pythagorean chart.

The destiny number from his name would look like this:

- E+L+O+N= 5+3+6+5= 19. Reduced to a single digit, 1+9= 10. Further reduced, 1+0=1
- R+E+E+V+E= 9+5+5+4+5= 28; 2+8=10; 1+0=1

- M+U+S+K= 4+3+1+2=10; 1+0=1
- Destiny number - 1+1+1= 3

Life path number from his birthday (28th June 1971):

- 2+8=10; 1+0= 1
- 0+6=6
- 1+9+7+1= 18; 1+8=9
- Life path number is 1+6+9= 16 (reduced to 7)

From these calculations, Elon's power number will be life path + destiny number, which is 7+3=10 (reduced to 1).

Not everyone has a double-digit power number. No matter what your power number is, you are special.

44 — The Master Healer

This power number combines and amplifies the vibrations of 8 and 4. It is a rare number in numerology and is fondly referred to as the master healer. If you fall into this group, you need time, balance, and a stable foundation to hone your innate talents and realize your true potential. 4 is the most detail-oriented power number in numerology, and 44 guarantees twice the detail, all geared towards success. You have prudence and extreme drive, which makes them fashion well-thought-out game plans for success in realizing their goals. You practice big picture visualization and have a good understanding of plans that lead to long-term success. You have a fondness for hierarchy and structure, coupled with a penchant for discipline and dedication. There are a number of magical powers of manifestation. Since this number reduces to the auspicious number 8, you are extremely lucky in life or anything to do with material wealth. You possess the Midas touch and attract abundance.

Sometimes you're susceptible to greed, especially when your focus on creating wealth supersedes other aspects of your life. Your family and love life are always in jeopardy. You might also be plagued by perfectionism paralysis because your intense desire to get your ducks in a row may just mean you never get to do much or take any steps.

All in all, this power number is the perfect blend of pragmatism, efficiency (4), balance, abundance, and realism (8). Seeing this number constantly is a sign from the divine that you should rid yourself of doubts concerning your future because you are already tuned to the frequency of abundance. It also signifies that you pay attention to the people around you since they may be channels for new opportunities.

55 — The Unconventional Leader

55 is the one that thinks outside the box, the mad scientist, so to speak. 55 is the fun and freedom-loving 5 paired with the independent and confident 1. This master number is the force that breaks new grounds, reaches new heights, and is a whirlwind to be reckoned with in terms of ambition and the desire for adventure.

If you are a 55, you are likely self-sufficient, outward-looking, and forward-thinking. There is never a dull moment with you. Although you prefer your own company, you can control the magnetism that draws others to you, like bees to honey.

Constantly seeing 55 signifies that it is time to let go of your past and be ready for the big shift that's about to occur in your life. 55 is a twin flame number, and seeing it means you should embrace the path of positive impact to enable you to meet your twin flame or other half. The number 55 is the "changes number" – and mostly appears to you when you are on the path of self-reinvention. You just need to be patient and wait out the changes that will happen soon. Start living in the present. The past is gone, and the future will handle itself.

66 — The Idealist

This power number characterizes the idealistic, creative, and optimistic idealist. 66 is extremely reliable. It reduces to 12, a number mystically associated with the boundaries of time and space. Whenever any core number reduces to 12, it means that time will be a major factor in the vibrations and energies of that number.

This power number is a number laden with feminine energy. 66 individuals are extremely nurturing and have a strong maternal instinct. Many of them need to care for something: a plant, pet, or person. As a 66 individual, the main focus of your existence is your home and relationships. There is little you wouldn't do to ensure they remain intact. You are also very in tune with nature and may find yourself involved in activities surrounding eco-conservation.

You have a tendency to care about and focus on others, usually to the detriment of yourself. In this case, balance is key, and the universe is trying to signal to you when you see this number to care for yourself to the same degree and with the same fervor with which you care for others.

Your perfectionist nature makes you a procrastinator. Alternatively, you may have a love-hate relationship with time. When you keep seeing this power number, the message is for you to prioritize and be mindful of your time and relationships in life. Learn time management skills, practice compassion, treasure the connections you have built, and sever ties with anyone who does not contribute to your happiness. The main goal is to cherish your peace of mind.

77 — The Master Helper

7 is naturally a number of introspection, contemplation, and self-reflection. It is one of the most spiritual and psychic numbers in numerology. This number enjoys solitude, so you can imagine just

how much of a loner a 77 individual is. However, the difference between 7 and 77 is that while 7 is concerned with self-care, 77 is relationship-oriented.

This master number combines the expression of the three master numbers and, where other power numbers lead through words, 77 leads via actions. 77 reduces to 14, which esoterically implies divine help or help in a time of need. 14 is a karmic number whose debt is as a result of past-life actions owing to an abuse of freedom. For this reason, it is vital for these 77 individuals to set themselves free and live unapologetically in the moment. A refusal to do this will keep them in a mercurial mood that stifles their creative streak.

From 14, power number 77 is further reduced to 5, which is concerned with breaking new ground and also embodies change. The main lesson for you as a 77 individual is to live happily in the now and face unexpected changes in the near future with a positive attitude. In terms of personality, you are very self-aware, and this quality only gets better with age. You are highly spiritual and charismatic. People tend to follow you or hold you in high regard in certain circles, even when you are not the official leader. You may enjoy solitude, but you are delightful when you decide to engage with others.

Constantly seeing 77 means that you are in line for a dose of spiritual awakening. It could also mean that you are being groomed for a leadership role. Understand that you have what it takes to be a great leader, even if that gene is dormant at the moment. Be ready to take on any leadership roles that come your way.

Another reason for seeing 77 is that major changes will take place in your life, which may seem negative at first but are for your greater good in the long run.

88 — The Master Entrepreneur

On an esoteric level, 8 symbolizes balance and infinity. The amplified version - 88 - has double the entrepreneurial capacity, eight times the energy of 11, four times the manifestation capacity of 22, and twice the disciplined, structured, and persistent energy of 44. Despite all of this, there is much more to 88 than material abundance.

As an 88 person, you are more focused and driven compared to 44, and even though both 88 and 44 appreciate solid plans in place, 88, as a more amplified version of 44, does not get caught up in materialism that 44 is bound to since it reduces to the spiritual number 7.

In matters of love, where 44 is clingy and dependent, 88 is more trusting and gives their significant other a lot of freedom. An 88 individual is the most objective person you will ever meet. The 88 is also a great judge of character and can see both sides of an argument clearly if compared with other power numbers.

Constantly seeing this power number is never a coincidence. It is a sign from the angels stating that all you wish for in life (not necessarily material in nature) is about to come your way. The only question now is how well equipped you are to handle this abundance. Seeing 88 is a gentle reminder to you to help people in need with the barrage of blessings coming your way. In the area of relationships, it advises that you show more love to your partner and initiate intimacy more than you are presently doing.

99 — The Master Humanitarian

This signifies humanitarianism, global awareness, consciousness, and tolerance. 99 reduces to 18, which in turn reduces to the single digit 9. 18 is a combination of the fiercely driven leader in 1 and the pragmatic visionary in 8, making this power number one you can depend on to make this world a better place.

Since 99 is the amplified version of the single digit 9, it means both the good and ugly traits of the number 9 are expressed in their most extreme forms. What is peculiar about this power number is the fact that it reduces back to itself, 9, which is not the same case with the other power numbers. As a result of this, individuals with 99 as their core number are more likely to focus on the energies of 9 in this lifetime.

99 symbolizes maturity, understanding, and the completion of a cycle. This number is similar to the introspective and internally-oriented 77 but possesses a high level of independence. 99 goes beyond the self-love expected from 1, the need for material wealth (2), the need to protect relationships and the home front (3, 4, 5), the need for a successful career (6), a love life (7), or the search for spirituality (8). 9 is concerned with universal love, encompassing all the elements important to all the numbers before it.

If you are a 99 individual, your main focus is on charitable acts since you are naturally giving of your time and energy. On the flip side, you can be more idealistic than the 44 and 66. Your Pollyanna-tinged lenses could also be laced with bitter cynicism, which makes you doubt yourself when you engage in charitable acts and question others' intentions when they act kindly toward you.

In love, 99 signals the end of loneliness. Love is in your near future. If you are in a relationship, this power number foretells a longer period of love and happiness. Your significant other will do anything to ensure you are loved and cared for. As number 9 signals finality, it also implies that people doing all they can to keep their relationship afloat will finally have the courage to break things off, move on, and start anew.

Chapter 5: Numerology and Astrology

Astrology is derived from the Latin root words "astro," meaning "star" and "logia," meaning "study of." This is an ancient science used to forecast human events and terrestrial affairs according to the placement or position of celestial bodies in the sky. Simply put, it is a science that studies the effects the cosmos has on human lives. Astrology has been in existence since the 2nd millennium BC. It was once considered a scholarly tradition by Greeks and Southeast Asians and is closely related to alchemy, medicine, astronomy, and metrology.

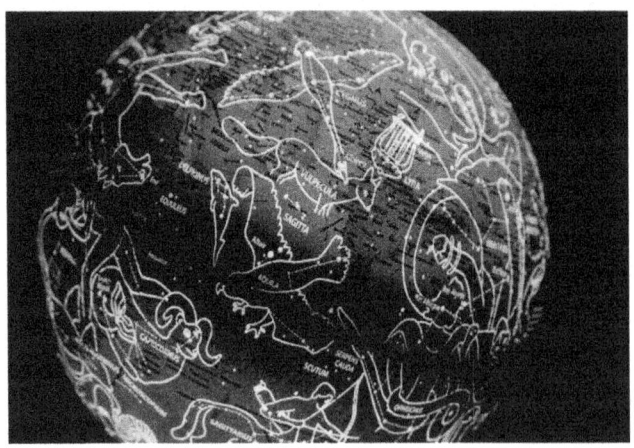

Astrology is often used interchangeably with astronomy. Both have common roots but are different from each other. While astrology is regarded as a pseudoscience, astronomy is the scientific study of the earth and every celestial body existing outside the earth's atmosphere and influence. Astrology studies the origins of these celestial bodies, their movements, and how they relate to or influence one another. According to popular poet and philosopher Ralph Waldo Emerson, astrology is astronomy brought down to earth and applied in the affairs of men."

The Link between Astrology and Numerology

Pythagoras discovered the relationship between both sciences in the 6th century BC – and both were used to make predictions. It is safe to say the Greek mathematician was the first person to find the connection between the stars, planets, and numbers after decades of intensive research.

Astrology is useless without numerical data concerning the person or event being investigated. This is because precise mathematical calculations need to be made to determine the position, angles, and heavenly bodies. In Vedic astrology, for instance, Siddhanta, a branch of Vedic astrology, uses numbers and arithmetic calculations to determine planetary positions, retrogressions, solar or lunar eclipses, etc.

Numerology charts study numbers in relation to planets, other celestial bodies, and horoscopes. All numbers are governed by certain planets, which allow these numbers (and people born under the influence of those numbers) to have certain personality traits. In Vedic astrology, the Vedic square is used to analyze the precise angles and positions of the planets and stars at the time of an individual's birth. The positions are then noted, vibrations of numbers written down, and these are then compared to present positions for predictive purposes or personality assessments.

Numerology and astrological readings reinforce each other in such a way that a higher meaning is deduced when both readings are combined. The fusion of astrology and numerology is called "astro-numerology" and is used in creating birth charts and horoscopes to help people find their meaning in life.

Numbers and planets are grouped based on the type of energy they possess, namely masculine and feminine (refer to the Tamil numerology chart in chapter two). The planets have numbers ascribed to them, and these numbers have specific vibrations and characteristics. These numbers are, in turn, linked to the zodiac signs to determine personality traits.

For instance, the sun is given the number 1. The sun is the king of the solar system and 1, the creator of all other numbers. Individuals with this number in their chart are assertive, independent, and rule the roost. The moon is linked to the number 2, which represents feminine energy, a pair, and the interdependence of two individuals. Number two individuals are peaceful, romantic, and sentimental. The fusion of numerology and astrology is used by many to name babies, pets, business ventures, and so on.

Pure scientists may dismiss numerology and astrology as groundless ramblings, but many scientists believed in the power of numbers, the planets, and the stars.

Hippocrates, the father of medicine, was a firm believer in the fact that a patient's astrological sign gave hints about their medical history and the diseases they were most predisposed to. Johannes Kepler, a German philosopher, mathematician extraordinaire, and pupil of the Danish astronomer, Tycho Brahe, believed strongly in the influence of celestial bodies on people and the Earth.

He went ahead to change the world by applying numbers in the formulation of the three laws of planetary motion, successfully applying mathematics, geometry, and physics to the study of the stars. Albert Einstein provided mathematical theories and descriptions concerning universal order and the machinations of the human psyche based on astrology and the vibrations given off by numbers.

From these explanations, it is clear to see how both metaphysical sciences influence, depend on, and complement one another. No astrologer worth their salt can properly plan or read a birth chart with a shoddy grasp of the meaning and symbols of numbers. Numerologists may not need to have an absolute understanding of astrology, but some basic knowledge of planetary influence will supplement their art.

1 — Ruled by the Sun (Zodiac Alter-Ego: Leo)

The sun is the ruling celestial body for individuals born on the 1st, 10th, 19th, or 28th of any given month. The sun is the king of the solar system, around which all other planets revolve. Any planet that gets too close to the sun deteriorates. According to Hindu scriptures, the sun obeys cosmic law, is home to our ancestors, and is the first in a line of the Vasus (dwelling places of consciousness). The sun is exalted in Aries, the first of the zodiac signs.

Like the lion, 1's are vivacious, authoritative, opinionated, and clear in their expressions. They enjoy the attention they get and have a difficult time changing their mindset or purpose. They love their freedom and march to the beat of their own drum. They care a great deal for others, make friends easily, and have no difficulty getting favors from people in positions of authority. They are blessed with good fortune, influence, courage, strong bodies, and more vitality than the average person.

A major defining characteristic is their love for luxury. They spend extravagantly on themselves and others and are notorious showoffs. A typical Leo has the latest and boldest fashion items the minute they hit the shelves. They also dislike criticism, so think long and hard before you fact-check or criticize a number 1. Try buttering them up with compliments before you drop your critique. Don't worry. They will listen because, deep down, the truth matters more to them than their own personal opinions. Like the sun, the number one is a source of illumination to others and is disciplined, practical, straightforward, and committed to serving humanity.

Budgeting and saving are two precautions to take. These are not entirely alien concepts, but they tend to avoid each other.

2—Ruled by the Moon (Zodiac Alter-Ego: Cancer)

The moon is the ruling celestial body of individuals born on the 2nd, 4th, 11th, 20th, and 29th of any given month. Those born on the 29th are the luckiest. The sun may be the chief celestial body, but the moon is essential for the survival of the earth and all its inhabitants. The moon reflects the sun's light via an alchemical process involving special gems on the moon's surface called "moon crystals" (chandra mukhi mani). The moon crystals have a medicinal effect on the planet, which is why healing plants and herbs thrive more at night under the light of the moon.

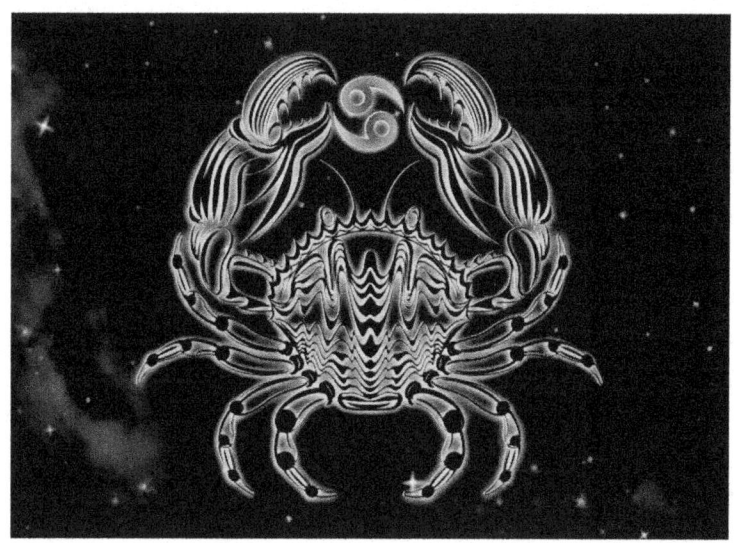

Though only 15% as strong as the sun, the moon has rays that effectively penetrate the soil, affecting plant life, moisture content, and growth from germination through to harvest. Science has also proven that plants fare better with rhythmic exposure to moonlight and are more robust when harvested in the last week of the lunar cycle. I guess Wiccans have been onto something their whole lives! This is the reason why an alternative name for the moon is "soma," or nectar.

The moon is a giant ball of feminine, nurturing, creative energy, much like the number 2, which is governed by it. People with psychic number two are sensitive and emotional, sensuous, romantic, and appreciative of art and beauty, traits which the zodiac sign of Cancer is known for. The moon governs cancer and is exalted in Taurus.

The moon's constant waxing and waning phases make people prone to mood swings and emotional instability. They go from happy and hopeful to moody and depressed in moments. Psychic number 2 enjoys solitude, but those born on the 11th take extra measures to self isolate. Number 2 individuals have a mucus-dominated disposition. The moon influences the left nostril, the left eye, the left-hand channels of the body, and the brain's right hemisphere.

Evolved number 2s always see through to the end whatever project they set their mind to. They are reserved by nature, but friendships are sacred. In case 2, you have a friend for life. Their docile nature is a magnet for narcissists and people who wish to take advantage of them. They are warriors fond of making the same mistakes over and over. Although they are very attractive, they have a huge amount of self-doubt and, as a result, fall prey to a little flattery.

3 — Ruled by Jupiter (Zodiac Alter-Ego: Sagittarius, Pisces)

Jupiter is the ruling celestial body for people born on the 3rd, 12th, 21st, or 30th of any given month and those with the destiny number 3. Those born on the 12th are the most fortunate. Those born on the 30th are usually the least fortunate.

Jupiter is a gigantic self-illuminating body that gives off more energy than it receives from the sun. It is the largest of all the planets in the solar system, and its size earned it the name "Guru" in Sanskrit, which means "remover of darkness" or "heavy." According to the Vedic scriptures, Jupiter is a planet representative of knowledge, hard work, righteousness, courage, boldness, and speech. Jupiter is exalted in cancer and associated with the Rigvedic deity Vachaspati, the god of eloquence.

Jupiter reigns over Pisces and Sagittarius and is exalted in Cancer. Jupiter rules over the ninth house of the birth chart (the house of fate) and is co-ruler of the 12th house (the house of the unconscious). As ruler of the house of fate, its position in the birth chart is of the utmost significance as it determines education, marriage, and childbirth. A female's birth chart can determine the lifespan, behavior, status, and character of her life partner. When Jupiter is positioned in opposition to the sun, Saturn, or Uranus, marriage is delayed or ends in divorce.

Number 3 individuals are popular, hard-working, dependable, ambitious, and self-confident. They are very future-oriented individuals who dislike working as subordinates; thus, they create opportunities for entrepreneurship. Like the Sagittarius star sign, 3s love to travel and are eager to meet as many people as they can within their lifespan. They have a strong sense of observation and logic, and their hard-working nature ensures that they are always busy with one thing or the other. They try to rest but usually can't switch their brains off. Like number 1, they value compliments and being appreciated for anything they do.

3s are blessed with the gift of the gab, even though their sense of humor might be offensive to many. Their short temper and assertive nature make them a lot of enemies, and as a result, they keep a small circle of friends. Not to worry, they are great friends since they are helpful and keep their promises.

4 — Ruled by Uranus (Zodiac Alter-Ego: Aquarius)

Uranus is the ruling celestial body of individuals born on the 4th, 13th, 22nd, or 31st of any month. In Scorpio, Uranus is exalted. The characteristics mentioned below also apply to people who have a destiny or name number of 4, although these qualities are more pronounced in individuals with a soul number of 4. 4 is the number associated with cosmic static integrity and is an ideally stable number. There are four seasons and four cardinal points. For example, many objects of esoteric significance have four sides or angles, for example, the mandala, the crucifix, and the square.

Individuals under its influence are illogical, dull, and lazy, with short attention spans. They often become detectives, spies, conspirators, or revolutionaries because of their aversion to work and their unconventionally genius ideas. Uranus causes fear, doubt, hostility, ignorance, and big plans that take an eternity to fulfill. This makes individuals under its influence work harder than most and, in the end, stack up bad karma that isn't good for them.

An evolved 4 is creative with artistic talents and is blessed with physical attractiveness, boldness, intelligence, and a highly secretive nature. Most of the time, in their endeavors, they side with the opposition or the underdog, which can create enemies. This is because they possess a specific viewpoint that enables them to see the truth inherent in all things. When Uranus is allied with Jupiter or Venus, individuals gain access to psychic sciences like tantra.

The unfavorable part of Uranus makes individuals selfish, arrogant, aggressive, and pessimistic. This, in turn, causes them opposition, humiliation, and other difficulties not easily diagnosed by medical means. In the worst cases, the individuals develop suicidal tendencies. Uranus is the day ruler of Aquarius and the 11th house (the house of friendship) on the birth chart. Friends of Aquarius include Virgo, Pisces, Gemini, and Sagittarius. Its enemies are Leo and Cancer.

Astrologers compare Uranus with smoke; it is amorphous but permeates every surface and crevice. It has the element of air. Because number 4 individuals are sensitized to the difference between good and evil, they have strong powers of judgment and are very doubtful and critical of others. They are also extremists; there is no middle ground for them. They either fiercely love or fiercely hate, but on the flip side, they are reliable, patient, and steadfast friends with large hearts. They are not interested in accumulating riches but give abundantly to the community and the needy.

5 — Ruled by Mercury (Zodiac Alter-Ego: Gemini, Virgo)

Mercury is the ruling celestial body of individuals born on the 5th, 14th, and 23rd of any month or whose name or destiny number adds up to 5. Those born on the 23rd are the luckiest, while the least fortunate are those born on the 14th. Mercury, the smallest planet in the solar system, is fondly called Kumar (youthful in Sanskrit) because of its evergreen nature. It is also called "Buddha" (intellect in Sanskrit).

Mercury is a gender-neutral celestial body associated with the element of earth. It influences the nervous and respiratory systems and intelligence, education, and eloquence. Mercury is a planet of extremes. They can be quite money-minded and materialistic on the one hand or disinterested in wealth accumulation and drawn to austere living on the other. This planet may be auspicious and benevolent, but its influence on individuals could make them cunning, deceitful, serious, and manipulative. However, 5s, just like the planet governing them, are forces of nature, attractive, fond of travel or adventure, eloquent, soft-spoken, and lovers of the arts.

4s have a quick wit and are broad-minded scholars. Their brains are never at rest. They are constantly trying to fill it with new information. They are jovial, impulsive, and very dedicated to consuming a lot of their energy to create a jolly atmosphere and make people happy. This usually backfires because no one is capable of pleasing everyone. Their impulsivity does not allow for long-term planning or lifelong friendships, even though they make friends very easily.

Their merchant nature predisposes them to take big risks, and some of them acquire wealth in this way. They are intuitive, adaptable, and have a clarity of expression that is envied by other signs. They are spendthrifts by nature and do not believe in only one source of income. Add this to their speculative nature and willingness to take risks, and you have a sign that's never in need of money.

Number 5 is always in a hurry. They value their time more than anything else. The best advice for 5 is to relax more. This helps them get over their intense and broody natures. They should also, under no circumstance, lose their jovial nature and sense of humor.

6—Ruled by Venus (Zodiac Alter-Ego: Taurus, Libra)

Venus is the ruling celestial body of individuals born on the 6th, 15th, and 24th of any given month. The 24th is the most fortunate of the 6. This also applies to people with destiny or name number of 6. 6s are romantic, active, sensual, and passionate as a result. Venus influences the reproductive organs, eyes, throat, chin, and kidneys. Venus-dominated individuals have doe eyes, beautifully proportioned bodies, and a lively yet graceful persona.

Venus governs men in a different way than it does women. The 6s have a mesmerizing magnetic personality. They are lovers of refined tastes and hobbies. Members of the opposite sex are easily drawn to them, and their social nature makes it easy for them to engage with a variety of people. They dislike sloppiness, disorder, and dirt.

It is easy for a 6 to learn the deeply guarded secrets of others, but their secretive nature makes them confidants you can trust. Trust them to enforce their will without coercion and to hide their anger under a deceptive smile. They love and desire companionship and despise solitude.

It is best to avoid planning revenge and stewing over past wrongs. This affects their nervous systems adversely. They are advised to avoid spicy foods, fats, oils, and sweet dishes. Weak periods are in April, October, and November when Venus is retrograde. Peak periods include April 20th through May 18th and September 21st through October 19th.

7—Ruled by Neptune (Zodiac Alter-Ego: Pisces)

Neptune is the ruling celestial body for individuals born on the 7th, 16th, and 25th of any given month. This also applies to people with a destiny or name number of 7. The qualities of Neptune are predominant in people with the psychic number 7. Neptune is exalted in Leo. It is gender-neutral, although many astrologers consider it feminine. Neptune is a deeply spiritual planet that bestows upon a 7 wisdom, non-attachment to worldly cares, lack of ambition, and a high dose of sensitivity.

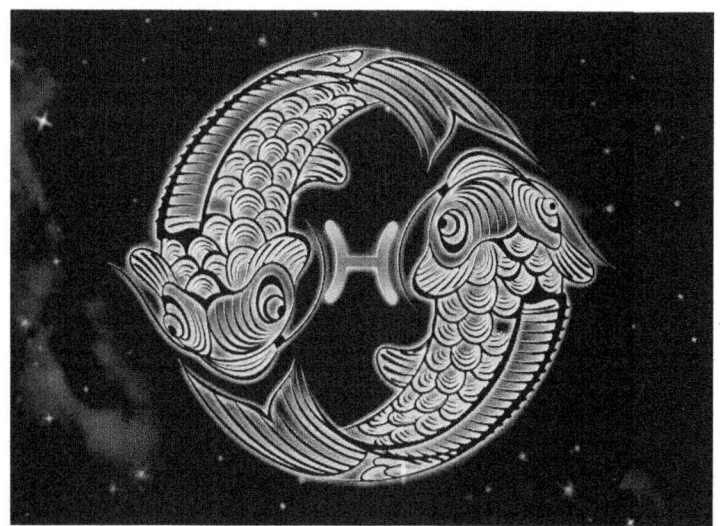

Neptune is more powerful at night and, when in a favorable position in the birth chart, gives seven psychic abilities such as healing through herbs, reiki, witchcraft, food, and occult sciences. 7s, like their zodiac counterparts Pisces, live in an imaginary world of their own making. They are quite intelligent, love debates, and have their own brand of logic. They are usually shabby or cosmopolitan in appearance. Their body chemistry is dominated by the element of air, and because of this, they are restless.

Neptune's allies are Mercury, Saturn, Venus, and Uranus. Jupiter is neutral, while the sun, moon, and Mars are their enemies. The negative influence of Neptune makes the 7 indecisive, moody, restless, and destructive. They make many mistakes and encounter a lot of failures in life. This failure is usually utilized as a steppingstone to their success.

With a Piscean, uncertainty is their stock in trade, but don't be fooled. There is a method to their madness and an order to their chaos. Many individuals become poets, arbitrators, writers, artists, scientists, and numerologists. The key is well-structured guidance to make their mark on the world. Individuals in this category are romantic, noble, kindhearted, and authentic. They live their lives unapologetically and without a care in the world. Space and freedom are deeply important to them, and this makes them advocates of social justice.

8—Ruled by Saturn (Zodiac Alter-Ego: Capricorn)

Saturn is the ruling celestial body of individuals born on the 8th, 17th, or 26th of any given month, as well as those with the name or destiny number 8. Saturn is the furthest planet in the solar system and is exalted in Libra.

When Saturn is in an unfavorable position in a birth chart, the individual under its influence becomes gloomy, greedy, and macabre. Saturn is the most destructive and disadvantageous of all the malefic planets. As the planet of darkness, it reigns supreme over the dark side of human nature and the awareness of right and wrong (the human conscience). If this planet is positively positioned in a natal chart, it will bring to its beneficiary wisdom, a sharp sense of right and wrong, sincerity, honesty, a long life, leadership, organizational abilities, a sense of authority, and leadership qualities.

Because Saturn rules over old age (like Mercury rules over youth), the Saturn subjects behave like older individuals and are more mature in appearance compared to their actual age. Saturn influences the hair, nails, teeth, skin, bones, skeleton, and nervous system. Saturn has allies in Neptune, Mercury, and Saturn. Jupiter is neutral, while the sun, moon, and Mars are their enemies.

8 is a number of determination and tenacity. They are hard-working people who accept the toughest challenges and surmount them. They prefer solitude, but when they decide to engage in social situations, communities, or other groups, they are sincere in their dealings. Even with their honest intentions, they are the most misunderstood by everyone, family and friends included. Their distinctive personas give them a very strong presence. It is easy to tell when an 8 (or a *Saturnine*) walks into a room because they subsume all other auras.

8 is unpredictable, lacks humor, and will never get your joke (so don't bother!) They feel very lonely at heart, and though their outward appearance looks menacing, in their hearts, they are fuzzy teddies who will jump through hoops and the fires of the underworld for their friends and loved ones.

9—Ruled by Mars (Zodiac Alter-Ego: Aries, Scorpio)

Mars is the ruling celestial body of individuals born on the 9th, 18th, or 27th of any given month. It also applies to people with a name or destiny number of 9. Those born on the 9th are tougher, rougher around the edges, but most fortunate. People born on the 27th are much gentler and more critical, while those born on the 18th have inner turmoil, selfishness and will become very quarrelsome in the future. Mars rules over Aries and Scorpio. It is exalted in Capricorn.

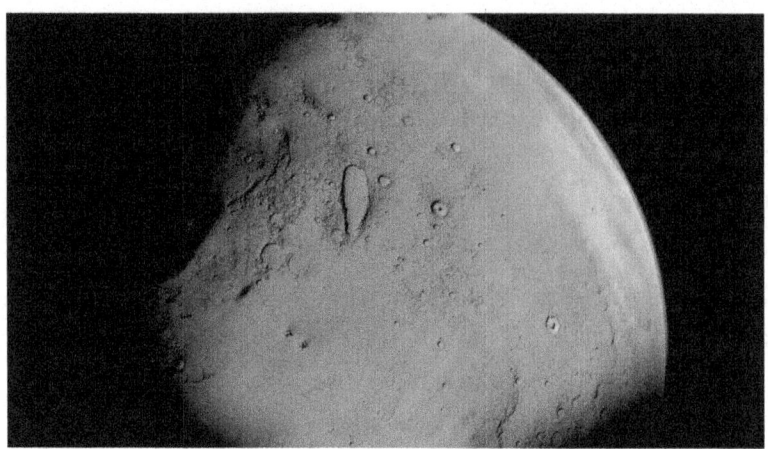

Mars is personified in Vedic texts as a strong figure with masculine energy. Mars is regarded as the commander in chief of all the planets in the solar system. The English word "martial" is derived from the qualities possessed by this planet. Duty, bravery, a sense of purpose, self-confidence, order, discipline, and courage.

Astrologers consider Mars to be a destructive planet because individuals under its influence are selfish and egotistical, putting their desires above others'. Its influence makes people headstrong, argumentative, fiery-tempered, lovers of dangerous weapons, cruel, restless, and violent. Mars also creates instability in romance and marital life when it dominates the 1st, 4th, 7th, or 10th house of their birth chart.

Martians and the number 9 are lovers of martial arts (no surprise there), politics, public speaking, hunting, sports, contests, and debates. They achieve the zenith of their power from 27 to 40 years of age. The Sun, Moon, and Jupiter are allies of Mars. Mercury is an enemy, while Venus, Saturn, Pluto, and Uranus are neutral.

Chapter 6: The Karmic Debt Numbers

The earliest mention of the word "karma" is found in the Rig Veda, an ancient compendium of Vedic Sanskrit hymns. Karma is derived from the Sanskrit word "karman," which literally translates to action, fate, or effect.

Karma is a concept in Hinduism and Buddhism that teaches how the sum of a person's deeds in previous and present lifetimes creates a system of actions and reactions that either impact or determine their fate in future lifetimes. This sum of a person's actions (beneficial or harmful) throughout a soul's reincarnated existence creates the cycle of birth-rebirth (samsara). In Vedic texts, the lord of Karma is the planet Saturn.

Karma is divided into three types:

> 1. **Sanchita**: Sanchita means "heaped together." Thus, this is the sum or collection of past karmas ready to be experienced after reincarnation.
>
> 2. **Prarabdha**: Karma is experienced by the body and forms a small part of Sanchita Karma.

3. **Agami:** Karma is formed from our actions here and now.

This universal law of karma is called the principle of cause and effect, and it governs all consciousness. It is important to know two facts. The first is that karma is different from fate. We all possess free will and are in charge of fashioning our destinies. The second is that not all karma is experienced in one lifetime. Some could accumulate to return in later incarnations. Humans are said to produce karma in four ways:

1. Words.
2. Thought.
3. Deeds performed personally.
4. Acts that others carry out as a result of our direction, instigation, or instruction.

Karma can only be repaid while we are alive. Death robs us of our power to act (Kriya Shakti) and our power to do (Kriya Mana). Hence, we can only wait until we are incarnated in another body to resolve our karma. Judging by this analogy, animals and infants are unable to create new karma since they are unable to distinguish between right and wrong.

Karma in Numerology

The question now is: what does karma have to do with numbers? The idea behind karma in numerology is that the soul carries both wisdom and challenges from events we faced or mistakes we made in previous lifetimes. These karmic conditions are revealed to us through the science of numbers.

Karmic Debt vs. Karmic Lessons

Both concepts are interwoven since they both concern karma from previous lifetimes. A karmic debt is an event or transgression that occurred in a past life that you are atoning for. On the other hand, a karmic lesson is a collection of situations, experiences, and themes from previous lifetimes that we didn't learn any lessons from. These situations keep repeating themselves until you learn something from them.

Karmic debts speak to the present challenges you face, while karmic lessons point to the tools missing in your life that could aid you in your quest to evolve. This follows the basic assumption that we are all souls, born to evolve towards higher states of enlightenment. In numerology, karmic debts are calculated differently from karmic lessons.

Karmic lessons are discovered by looking at the full letters of your given name as stated on your birth certificate and finding out which numbers are missing. To calculate the karmic lesson number for Clarence John Smith, these are the numerical values of the name according to Pythagorean numerology:

- $C - L - A - R - E - N - C - E = 3 - 3 - 1 - 9 - 5 - 5 - 3 - 5$
- $J - O - H - N = 1 - 6 - 8 - 5$
- $S - M - I - T - H = 1 - 4 - 9 - 2 - 8$

From the example, it is clear that some numbers appear more than once. The only number missing is the number 7. So, for Clarence, his karmic lesson is 7.

Signs You Have Karmic Debt

1. You find yourself catering to or caring for certain kinds of people. This may be karma's influence on you as a form of payback for misdeeds or selfishness in a past life.

2. You are always facing or struggling with problematic patterns or cycles. It could be anything from abusive relationships to financial debt. This would point toward a

past life of excessive indulgence in either sex or material gain.

3. You experience patterns of behavior you can't explain. There is a saying that goes, "*That which cannot be explained in this lifetime is certainly rooted in a past life.*" This is often the only way to make sense of irrational phobias we may have or patterns of behavior we are sure were not picked up from our present existence. It may all stem from a previous life, whether it is a fear of fire, an aversion to happiness, or certain foods.

4. There are unlimited opportunities for mastery in this lifetime. You may try to skirt around or ignore the karmic issues you face. Failure to address these debts keeps them in your life until you settle the score and gain mastery of the lesson your karma is trying to teach you. Like any vicious cycle, unfulfilled karmic debts feel like a trap and can transform into dangerous habits if you fail to develop self-awareness. Instead of addressing your debts, you just keep piling on more with time.

5. You have at least one karmic relationship in this life. A karmic relationship is one that is undeniably strong and fulfilling on the one hand but emotionally draining, unpleasant, and toxic on the other. This points to a debt you owe the person from a previous lifetime.

6. Karmic numbers are present in your birth chart. These are the most obvious, and a full explanation will be given below.

What Numbers Carry Karmic Debt?

The karmic debt numbers are 13, 14, 16, and 19. They are considered only when they appear in any of your core numbers, namely:

- **Life Path Number:** Calculated from the date of birth. Life path numbers that add up to any of the karmic digits or include numbers 1, 4, 5, and 7 since they are the single-digit reductions of the double-digit karmic numbers.

- **Soul Urge Number:** Calculated from the addition of consonants in your name.

- **Personality Numbers:** From the numbers in your birthday and month.

- **Expression Number:** From the sum of digits that make up your name.

Another method of calculating your karmic number is by adding together your name number and life path number. Note that the name used must be your birth name as it is written on your birth certificate. Do not use pet names or any adopted names. Once you accept and begin to understand the debts you must atone for in this lifetime, you have the rare opportunity to break the cycle and quit repeating the same mistakes again and again. This will finally set your soul free. Some people do not have a karmic debt number, but this is very rare.

The absence of a karmic number simply means your soul journey has a different meaning, one not tied to the concept of repaying past life debts. But if you do have one, it's not a curse or anything to be afraid of. Whether you have a karmic debt number or not, the fact remains that we are all fighting our personal battles or struggling with one pattern or the other. Below is a list of karmic debt numbers and how you can use them as a steppingstone for personal growth. Each of these karmic debt numbers has a specific significance, outlines a specific level of hardship in this lifetime, and teaches a particular type of lesson. An individual can have more than one karmic debt number, and I will address each of these numbers and explain their lessons.

Karmic Debt Number 13/4

A karmic debt of 13 or a life path of 4 implies abuse of morals for personal gain in a past life. This karmic debt signifies that you were probably lazy and self-indulgent in a previous life or that you had no self-control.

Laziness comes naturally to most humans, but this is especially true for those with this karmic number. Your aversion to work in a previous life prevented you from completing or attempting tasks. Staving off a lazy attitude is the most prominent life lesson associated with this number.

This is why people with 13 usually encounter numerous roadblocks and have to put in more effort than most to achieve success. How then does one work off this debt? Accountability. Yes, you will need to hold yourself responsible for your actions. Your purpose is to learn that there is no substitute for hard work.

When it comes to self-indulgence, the appearance of this karmic debt number is a result of the fact that you achieved most or all of your success using the sweat or effort of others in your previous life. You were a pro at avoiding responsibilities and found joy in taking credit for their effort rather than your own.

Karmic number 13/4 demands that you set your sights on aspects of life unrelated to pleasure. This karmic debt number may also point to an addiction of some kind in a past life for the sake of personal gain. If the same habit rings true in this lifetime, then you need to desist immediately.

Now let's talk about lacking self-control. Because of self-indulgence, you naturally have no control whatsoever over your impulses, be they your temperament, emotions, sexual desires, or love for intoxicants. In the past, you indulged in the basest urges of your mind without a care for how they affected your health, state of mind, or how they affected others around you. This debt number urges you to develop healthier habits (which help you live better in the long run) and improve your self-control because that will help you achieve your dreams in this life.

While maintaining discipline and order in your life, understand that there is always room to let new and creative ideas flow in from any source. Learn to be vulnerable around others. Don't be so set in your ways that you gloss over a fantastic idea simply because of your idealistic tendencies or lack of willingness to put in any effort.

Karmic Debt Number 14/5

A karmic debt number of 14 or a life path of 5 implies abuse of freedom in a past life or a problem with you relinquishing control or power to others, sometimes to the detriment of your wellbeing. This karmic debt number concerns independence, personal power, and self-direction. The main messages contained in the number 14 are fear and hope.

Individuals in this category of karmic debt suffer from escapism and wanderlust. As a result, focus does not come easily to them, and this is rooted in the number 5 (the reduced number 14) in their numerology chart. 5 has an adventurous spirit and has the habit of dumping people they know in favor of someone new and interesting. Your mission in this lifetime? Work through and get rid of the shiny-new-toy syndrome you have. Cultivate and invest in yourself, your health, finances, and present relationships because quality trumps quantity at any given time.

Rein in your fear. On the flip side of escapism and adventure is paralyzing fear. 5s and 14s may be courageous in the face of adventure, but beneath all that bravado is undiluted fear. This is because escapism presents its own unique brand of challenges that manifest in various forms, like the fear of escapism itself and the knowledge that excessive indulgence may bring you harm. There's also the fear of the unknown, drawn from the fact that you find commitment unappealing. You are constantly afraid of being so poor or helpless that you are at the mercy of others. The solution to this is to find a way to confront those fears head-on. Worrying won't solve your problems.

Karmic Number 16/7

A karmic debt number of 16 or a life path number of 7 implies a vain nature and an inflated ego that connects all of your previous lives to the present one. This means that, in the past, your arrogant nature caused a great deal of torment to those around you. A quote by Benjamin Franklin says, *"A man wrapped up in himself makes a very tiny bundle."* With the number 16/7, your past life was probably riddled with events where your sense of self-importance was used for non-constructive purposes, which is why your debt seeks to deflate your ego and keep you in touch with your inner self. This group needs to learn humility and how to drop bad habits to have a fresh, great beginning.

Humility is one karmic debt of ego that is one of the most difficult to overcome because it requires an endless cycle of deaths and rebirths (samsara) to gain humility and prove yourself worthy with each incarnation. Like the phoenix rising from the ashes, you must let go of old and harmful patterns to give way to a newer and more reformed version of yourself.

16/7 also implies transgressions regarding love and relationships in a previous lifetime. This can occur as a repetitive string of relationships where you either break others' hearts or get your heart broken. To address this karmic cycle, there is a need for you to remain mindful in your day-to-day activities and commit to connecting with others. When you start to become more thoughtful and self-aware, you think more about how your words might affect others and, as such, put more thought into them.

You have to let go of your bad habits to allow new and better energy to flow in. Humans naturally have an ego. It's a given. It is hard for many to admit the battles they fight in this lifetime. Why do you think therapy is pricey? With ego problems that have transcended lifetimes, handling the situation is even direr. You probably have a grand plan laid out for your life by a particular age, only for life to toss a monkey wrench and make a caricature of all your grand schemes. The lesson taught by this karmic number is flexibility and adaptability when faced with life's challenges.

It is difficult, if not downright impossible, for you to cultivate meaningful relationships with others. You find it hard to be vulnerable toward other people. Your pride never lets you ask for company either – and for this reason, you come across as pompous and self-absorbed. Because of a lack of social skills and an absence of close relationships, you are often misunderstood by people. Those with the typical number 7 (reduced to 16) are often thought to be unapproachable. Your body language is closed off, and your smiles come as often as it takes a comet to appear in the sky. You do a great job of showing others that you do not care about their opinion of you, so you make rash decisions that sabotage relationships you already have and new ones that are in the formation stages.

Do things differently in this lifetime. Instead of burning bridges like you usually would, expand your intuition and open yourself up to new paths, influences, ideas, and people. Practice listening to others and nurturing your relationships. You will find yourself surrounded by people who genuinely love and care for you with time.

Karmic Debt Number 19/1

A karmic number of 19, or a life path of 1, points to you having lived a narcissistic, manipulative, and selfish nature in a past life. You cared more about your assets, talents, and outward appearance. You also looked down on others, using them only to help you get ahead. You may have also been a cruel slave driver, punishing your subordinates and others of a lower social class than you

Debt number 19 is heavily linked to the abuse of power in a previous life. This selfish attitude has carried over to this lifetime, making you still turn down your nose at others. The lesson taught by 19 is the importance of focusing your attention outward and towards others instead of inwards and towards yourself. Refusal to acknowledge this debt can quickly turn your life into a self-imposed prison sentence until you recognize the importance of independence and the value of interdependence. With 19/1, you quickly realize that no man is an island. We all need each other to survive.

The superficial tendencies in the past that led to this debt amount teach three main lessons. One lesson is about shedding your pride. Like number 1 (reduced to 19), individuals in this category are very self-reliant and a bit of a know-it-all. They enjoy their own company, resolve all their issues alone, and do not accept or appreciate advice from anyone but themselves. Their self-realized ideals may be great, but they are bound to make a lot of mistakes that they find hard to forgive themselves for. The sooner they shed their pride, one-man-army mentality, and self-imposed independence, accepting that true balance comes from letting others in, the quicker they achieve success.

If you have a karmic debt of 19/1, do not be afraid or ashamed of what people will think when you ask for help. What's the worst that could happen? They refuse, right? But not everyone will refuse you, so there is nothing to worry about. Keep in mind that it is easier to stand on your own two feet while holding onto the hand of another for support and friendship.

Another lesson is being of service to others. It's possible that you were blessed with wealth and a variety of talents in a previous life, which you used to enrich and advance yourself. 19 comprises 1- signaling the genesis or beginning and 9-the end of a cycle or completion. Your karmic journey is concerned with all that is left in the middle. Learn to support others in any way you can and accept support when it is offered to you. Do not let your obstinate nature get in the way of the help you desperately need. After all, we can often learn to face our own inner turmoil through deeper connections with others.

Finally, there's the lesson of independence. In this lifetime, you must work to gain that which you want. It will be a struggle for someone who was a bully in a past life to work for something they desire and not snatch it from someone else. Avoid the temptation to manipulate people by double-checking if you really need or simply want something. When you learn to prioritize, you find that you can get by with what little you have. You may face challenges such as a secret lack of self-esteem or over-reliance on your partner or loved ones.

Chapter 7: Your Birthday Number

The birthday number is one of the five core numbers in the numerology chart. The others include:

- Life path number
- Expression number
- Soul urge number
- Personality number

The birthday number is derived from your date of birth (without the year), and it reveals the naturally unique abilities you possess as a human being. Each date of birth has its own sense of power and vibration. It is no coincidence that you were born on a specific day, in a specific month, in a particular year.

Numerologists believe that our souls select our birthdays, and these dates hold infinite power as they are aligned with cosmic forces that shape our natures and guide us through life. Unlike other core numbers, birthday numbers are not reduced to a single digit during a reading because each day has peculiar traits, strengths, and weaknesses attached to it. Your birthday number may be regarded as the least significant of all your core numbers, but it remains one of the most specific, describing the personality traits and flaws you possess to a great extent. This number describes your functioning capacity as a person, telling us how and why you do the things you do.

Calculating Your Birthday Number

This is the easiest core number to calculate. Your day of birth is all you need. For instance, if Jessica was born on the 11th of March, her birthday number is 11.

For double-digit birthday numbers, certain numerologists analyze their single-digit values (post-reduction). For instance, someone born on the 17th will definitely have 17 as their birthday number, but the numerologist will take the reduced digit 8 (1+7) into consideration. It is, however, important to understand that while numbers like 17 and 26, for instance, may have the same reduced single-digit value, the expression of traits will certainly differ.

17, for instance, combines the assertive, confident, and obstinate number 1 with the intellectual, insightful, yet solitary number 7. While 26 combines the gentle, sensitive, diplomatic 2 with the creative, nurturing, and self-sacrificing 6. Knowledge of this number helps you understand your positive traits and helps you work towards minimizing or totally eliminating the negative ones.

Below is a list of all the birth numbers and their dominant personality traits, from numbers 1 through 31.

- (1)

    You are a pioneer, an initiator with an energetic and creative personality. A natural leader of the pack, you play by your own rules because you have what it takes to carry out your plans. You have excellent business instincts, and you play to win. You are a master at using knowledge for a specific purpose. You are also a key source of influence and motivation for others.

Weaknesses

• You have an iron will. Your strong sense of what you like and dislike does not win you many friends.

• Your extreme need for independence and your domineering attitude make you a difficult person to work with or for. It's not like you mind anyway, since you dislike the restrictions that come with working with others.

• Anger and frustration come to the fore when things do not go the way you like them. Your favorite words are "I," "Yes," and "Now," in no particular order.

Ideal Professions

1 can succeed anywhere, but for them to truly shine like the alphas they are, they must be placed in work environments where routine and monotony do not exist. Their quick wit and flexible minds demand situations that will involve making spur-of-the-moment decisions and challenge their ingenuity to find ways to work around impossible situations.

1 is pleased to create reliable irrigation in the Sahara, design an automobile, create an impossibly catchy advert, or persuade a frugal businessman to buy a multimillion-dollar house. They would never thrive with jobs that involve, say, a cashier in a mall with fixed prices for goods, a toll booth collector, or even worse, a frozen pea tester.

Famous 1's: Dr. Phil, Justin Bieber, Penn Badgley, Missy Elliot

- (2)

As a diplomat and peacemaker, you are everything I am not. That is what makes you the Robin to their Batman. You are emotional, sensitive, intuitive, and in tune with your environment. Nothing escapes your attention, even if you don't talk about it. You are highly adaptable, affectionate, and warm and demand the same measure of affection from your loved ones.

Your family is very important to you. You thrive in a harmonious environment and love being made to feel safe and secure. You excel at continuing a project rather than starting it and work best with partnerships. Unlike someone who enjoys being on stage, you are content being the power behind the throne. You may not get all the accolades that are due to you, but that does not change the fact that you are indispensable in any endeavor.

Weaknesses

- Your extreme attention to detail and your environment can sometimes leave you stressed and high-spirited.

- Your emotional nature makes you prone to manipulation and leaves you vulnerable to people who tend to take you for granted.

- You suffer from a lack of self-confidence and are prone to bouts of depression.

Ideal Professions

Your talents are best concentrated in any field of endeavor that highlights your diplomatic skills. Human relations, business communication, legislation in private companies, and political ambassadorship. You will also fare well in the fields of medicine, art, civil service, and education.

Famous 2's: Ina Garten, Bon Jovi, Donatella Versace, and Dwayne "The Rock" Johnson.

- (3)

An enthusiastic and creative soul with the gift of garb. A 3 will talk their way out of a fight and take their opponents to lunch soon after. These smooth operators are the most charming and witty individuals you will ever meet. There is never a dull moment with them. They are highly imaginative individuals who have no problem attracting romantic interest. They always have a full social calendar that leaves others wondering how they never get burned out. They are also magnets for luck and abundance.

Weaknesses

- Your sense of imagination keeps you perpetually in your own little world. You are far from being realistic.

- You have a serious case of leaky pockets. Your spending abilities leave a lot to be desired.

- Your eternal optimism and childish innocence make you vulnerable to manipulators and narcissists.

- Your creative mind is eternally chaotic – you never finish anything you start.

Ideal Professions

Any area of creativity will work. 3 will do well as an artist, writer, poet, or actor. Sports or science will suit them too.

Famous 3's: Mel Gibson, Martha Stewart, Kendall Jenner, Tiffany Haddish

- (4)

4s are the salt of the earth. Diligent, loyal, conservative, and precise, the typical 4 is relied upon to manage and organize. They are not given to hurried or pie in the sky solutions; rather, they are ambush predators. With patience second to none, they will sit and wait, persevering until they "pounce," achieving their goals. 4s are always indispensable and in demand because they can fit into any endeavor and would not hesitate to tread where others have failed and come out successful.

Weaknesses

• Rigidity or inflexibility of thought makes you lose out on opportunities.

• Conservative beliefs and an emphasis on routine could make these individuals boring to be around.

Ideal professions

All professions in the world need a 4. They are required in areas where patience, responsibility, attention to detail, and organization are required. 4s do not merely work for monetary gain but truly enjoy their jobs.

Famous 4's: Audrey Hepburn, Heath Ledger, Barack Obama, Megan Markle.

- **(5)**

The only thing more important than freedom to a 5 is money, which, ironically, is one of the requirements to enjoy freedom. Lovers of adventure, change, and travel, they are thrill-seekers and adrenaline junkies who are always on a quest of some sort. They are highly adaptable individuals, gifted communicators, and creatives who come up with last-minute solutions to problems.

Weaknesses

• Your wanderlust makes you irresponsible and averse to discipline.

- You can be overconfident and obstinate, especially when you feel there are too many restrictions imposed on you.

- Impatient, impulsive, and prone to overindulgence in sex, food, and intoxicants.

Ideal Professions

Any job that requires you to be on the go or has flexible hours is ideal. Digital nomad jobs like website development, drop-shipping, blogging, digital marketing, freelance jobs, photography, etc. Sales is also a good option for you due to your sound communication skills.

Famous 5's: Christiano Ronaldo, Pharrell Williams, Tilda Swinton, Neymar

- **(6)**

This kind, compassionate, self-sacrificing caretaker is the mayor of the middle ground. They know how to strike a compromise and settle disputes effectively like no other. They are family-oriented and have a considerable measure of artistic flair. Their sense of responsibility and devotion keeps them focused in the area of relationships.

Weaknesses

- Being everyone's shoulder to cry on could leave you burnt out emotionally and physically.

- Your self-esteem problems leave you vulnerable to praise and flattery, which could lead you to make awful decisions to please others.

- Prone to extremes in sentimentality and sensitivity. You are either bawling your eyes out or laughing at the top of your lungs.

Ideal Professions

6's are the best caregivers you will find. Jobs that are suited to caring for people make them gravitate towards fields like alternative healing, health and mental therapy, social service, medicine, nursing, teaching, etc.

- (7)

These seekers of truth and wisdom have a mind as sharp as a samurai sword and as flexible as graphene. They are not given to emotional outbursts and have a balanced view of life. They are also unafraid of unforeseen circumstances, not because they are prepared, but because they will readily adapt and come out on top. 7 has excellent intuition and a strong interest in the metaphysical, scientific, and technical. You work methodically and finish whatever you start.

Weaknesses

- Emotions are uncharted territory for you. You are sensitive and feel deeply but find it hard to express yourself to others.

- 7s do not hesitate to use the word "no" freely. This is as a result of their cold, self-centered and analytical minds, which makes them very cynical.

Ideal Professions

They are more improvisers than solo performers or team players. 7 is best suited for jobs that require rhythmic activity and require rapid-fire decision making and big picture visualization, such as law enforcement, financial management, law enforcement, etc. Your ability to control your emotions also makes you suited for emergency medicine, surgery, professional coaching, athletes, etc.

Famous 7's: Paul Rand, Anna Kournikova, Charles Dickens, Jackie Chan.

- (8)

Born leaders, efficient managers with a knack for business and a penchant for making money, 8 is daring, original, competitive, ambitious, and goal-oriented. 8 can be compared to a pit bull. They are high-energy, self-confident people who will challenge you (and themselves) every step of the way, but when they sink their teeth into a project, they play to win. 8s have a presence so powerful it can be intimidating to others.

Weaknesses

- Greed that stems from over-ambition.

- A domineering attitude. 8 does not take kindly to signs of weakness from themselves or others.

- Heavy spending and a tendency to be show-offs.

Ideal Professions

8s are fashioned to create gold from silt. They can work anywhere but are suited to managerial roles, independent contractors, or entrepreneurs. They can also be found in business, industry, science, and entertainment.

Famous 8's: John D Rockefeller, Mauricio Macri, John Grisham, Gordon Ramsey

- (9)

The perfect combination of pragmatism and romantic idealism, 9 can dream of a life of luxury or the manna from heaven while flipping burgers at a diner to make ends meet. They are firm believers in doing what they can today while waiting for a brighter tomorrow. They have broad-minded thinking, are effective communicators, and can relate well with others. Their humanitarian streak ensures that they constantly strive to make the world a better place. They always attract money from unlikely sources and are known to have a stroke of luck.

Weaknesses

• A penchant for melodrama when expressing your feelings.

• Revenge-driven and has a difficult time forgiving or letting go of past wrongs.

Ideal Professions

Their calm, adaptable, and helpful nature makes them suitable for jobs with stability and consistency, such as librarians, recreational therapists, caretakers, teachers, and psychologists.

Famous 9's: Natalie Portman, Adam Sandler, Catherine (Duchess of Cambridge).

- **(10)**

Highly ambitious, independent, and intuitive, you have the uncanny ability to reinvent yourself no matter how many trials you face. You are also optimistic, creative, and authentic, with a passion for inspiring others. You are a loyal and devoted partner and friend.

Weaknesses

• Like number 1, you dislike details, so you tend to begin projects but leave them to others to finish them.

• You enjoy the thrill of the hunt and tend to suffer intense waves of jealousy over the success of others.

• Routines are the quickest way to frustrate you. You become dull and even fall ill when exposed to drudgery.

Ideal Professions

Team leaders in any field, jobs that require constant risk, speed, and heroics (formula 1 racer, fireman, stunt double, test pilot, police officer).

Famous 10's: Nikola Tesla, Judy Garland, Karl Lagerfield, Sofia Vergara

- **(11)**

Idealistic, with intuition so keen they are called the anatomists of the human soul, 11s understand people so well they can understand words unsaid and guess hidden intentions. You have a gift for sensitizing people toward certain pursuits, usually philosophical or idealistic. You are drawn to nature and are a lover of animals, great and small. You require a balanced lifestyle because, though you have the capacity for leadership, you prefer either to point the way to discovery or become an example others can emulate.

Weaknesses

- Your emotional and sensitive nature makes you easily hurt by the criticism of others.

- You are more intuitive and rational, which gives you a flair for the dramatic.

- You tend to live your life according to the wishes of others instead of your own because you care too much about what others think.

Ideal Professions

Jobs that require intuition and include the role of advisor are best suited for you. So, you will fare well in guidance counseling, academia, scientific research, statistics, health/nutrition advice, etc.

Famous 11's: Jennifer Aniston, Amitabh Bachchan, Thomas Edison, Didier Drogba

- (12)

Brimming with talent, originality, and vitality, 12 is the life and soul of any gathering and the very personification of a good time. You are a child at heart who is blessed with an impressive vocabulary and a wide knowledge of various subjects. Your amiable personality brings you friends from all walks of life.

Weaknesses

- The tendency to focus energy on trivial matters and people.

- You may be talented in making lemonade from lemons, but you are prone to moodiness and self-pity.

- Your varied interests may imply that sometimes you spread yourself too thin: a jack of all trades and master of none.

Ideal Professions

12 has talents suited to a variety of professions, but it is important for them to choose their vocations in the same way one would choose a spouse. They need to work in a field they are passionate about in order to give it all their energy. Money is not their inspiration to work.

Famous 12's: Jeff Bezos, Swami Vivekananda, Charles Darwin, Abraham Lincoln.

- (13)

Solid and practical, 13 is a lover of family, tradition, and community. You have an eye for detail and possess clarity of thought. You have a lot of creative ideas seeking an avenue for expression. You appreciate nature, design, beauty, and animals. You are an energetic, hard worker who is not afraid to share your opinions. You have a finely tuned sixth sense which either annoys or amazes people you come into contact with.

Weaknesses

• Your ability to apply yourself to long hours of work can leave you burnt out. On the flip side, you may feel you have not found the work you are meant to do, so you tend to wander from job to job, relationship to relationship, unable to apply yourself to any.

• You have an established routine and, as such, refuse to give way to newer creative ideas, even when it's obvious your method takes forever to get things done.

Ideal Professions

You are not predisposed to a particular line of work. You tend to do whatever it is that interests you and excel at it.

Famous 13's: Robbie Williams, Liam Hemsworth, Alfred Hitchcock, Tyler Perry

• (14)

An adventurer with a magnetic personality, a rebellious streak, and a dislike for conventions, 14 always has a bag packed and ready to go. You are easily bored and need to be stimulated constantly to feel alive. You are famous for your spur-of-the-moment decisions. You are good with words, popular in social circles, and a wonderful catch as a romantic partner (if the person gets your attention and holds it long enough).

Weaknesses

• Your restless nature ensures that you never stick to one thing, be it a profession, relationship, or dwelling.

• Beneath your love for change and excitement is insecurity, such that manifests in your life as mood swings and rash decision making.

- You tend to overindulge in sex, drugs, food, or alcohol as a means of escape.

Ideal Professions

14 is extremely talented and versatile. They display competence in any field or endeavor they set their minds to. But they are best suited to jobs involving excitement and change. The more daring they are, the better. They will do well as SWAT team members, bomb explosion experts, aerospace engineers, war correspondents, adventure filmmakers, etc.

Famous 14's: Albert Einstein, Mark Zuckerberg, Earvin "Magic" Johnson, Condoleezza Rice.

- **(15)**

Highly creative, with a gift for languages and a strong inclination towards the visual arts, 15 is independent, very sensitive, and sympathetic to the plight of others. They are devoted to friends and family and can be very self-sacrificing, even to the point of self-harm. However, their multi-talented nature includes sharp business and financial acumen, which ensures their success in life.

Weaknesses

- You do not react well to criticism and get hurt easily because of your sensitive nature.

- People tend to take advantage of your help and presence for their selfish gain because of your trusting nature.

Ideal Professions

You are drawn towards fields where support and care for others are essential. However, since you are always seeking validation from others, you will do well in the fields of healthcare, social service, sports as a coach or personal trainer, physical therapist, or home health aide.

Famous 15's: Martin Luther King Jr., Agatha Christie, Emma Watson, Prince Harry (Duke of Sussex).

- **(16)**

The perceptive, intuitive, inquisitive, and extremely analytical 16 can spot a phony from two miles away. They can tell lies from truth faster than you can flip a pancake. They dislike surprises, large crowds, noisy atmospheres, and loose ends. Their analytical mind and unparalleled levels of concentration allow them to gain depths of knowledge in various fields. You are drawn to the metaphysical and philosophical. Although when you put yourself out there, you are great company and easy to relate with.

Weaknesses

- You have two mood ranges; impractical and dreamy or moody and bitter. This makes you feel alone at heart, pessimistic and depressed.

- Your introverted and inflexible nature keeps you from adapting easily to change.

Ideal Professions

16s work hard to become perfectionists in their chosen field, but they are attracted to extremes. You either find them in something as profound as spirituality or metaphysical pursuits or in something as tedious and mundane as computer programming, coding, tax law, accounting, etc.

Famous 16's: Madonna, Abel Makkonen, Tesfaye alias "The Weekend," Pope Benedict XVI, Geronimo.

- **(17)**

The highly independent, ambitious 17 is blessed with sound judgment that makes them a whiz at business and finance. Like the 8, which is a reduced form of the 17, they are efficient managers and organizers, skilled at seeing the big picture. Your capabilities are greater than those of the average person, and you know this all too well. Do NOT attempt to deceive a 17. They have the memory of an elephant. They are also not given to gossip and hearsay. As far as the typical 17 is concerned, if there is no supporting evidence, something does not exist.

Weaknesses

- Your over-inflated ego and high expectations of yourself tend to cloud your judgment. This prevents you from handing over authority and delegating to others. You constantly micromanage others and feel no one can do a better job than you do.

- Your love for status and the lavish life encourage abysmally poor saving habits.

- You have a hard time handling failure. It always feels like a blow to your ego.

Ideal Professions

17, like 8, was born to make money. They can make it out of thin air. They fare well in positions that give them some form of authority over others, regardless of the field. Often, they are managers, team leaders, coordinators, and administrators.

Famous 17s: Michelle Obama, Al Capone, Victoria Beckham, Venus Williams

- (18)

The broad-minded 18s are pioneers in their field, admired by many with a knack for organizing and inspiring people. They are drawn towards the arts. It is little wonder that many artists are found in this category. You have a sharp mind with the ability to assimilate vast amounts of information, like a memory card, only you have no limits. Despite your calm, aristocratic appearance, your deepest satisfaction lies in getting your hands dirty in service to humanity.

Weaknesses

- Your luck with money makes you an impulsive spender. Also, people tend to borrow large sums of money from you with the intention of paying it back.

- You are usually prone to extremes in behavior. It's either you are extremely wealthy or extremely envious of another's success; highly intuitive or insanely oblivious of your surroundings.

- Violent temper tantrums alienate you from friends or loved ones and cause difficulty in forgiving others.

- They feel a high level of insecurity despite their dedication to work and their notable intelligence.

Ideal Professions

18 is a late bloomer who tends to have a finger in every pie before settling on one. Usually, they try out a lot of professions but are ideally suited to the fields of religion, law, public and social work, and politics.

Famous 18s: Jada Pinkett Smith, Sia, Steven Spielberg, Pep Guardiola, Pope John Paul II

- **(19)**

The highly independent, self-sufficient maverick is personified by 19. They have high levels of endurance and responsibility, but their need for self-sustainability is so extreme it trumps every other need they may have. They are hard workers and indispensable in every field or endeavor. People are attracted to them because of the efficiency with which they perform their duties. You are highly idealistic, sensitive, and find yourself smack-dab in the middle of dramatic situations, though you have no issues keeping your cool.

Weaknesses

- Failure makes you bitter and negative.
- You have problems controlling your temper, but the good part is that you don't stay mad for too long.
- You tend to be nervous when faced with difficult situations.
- You have bad spending habits.

Ideal Professions

You have what it takes to be a star in virtually any field since you are able to work both alone and as a team player. You are, however, more attracted to jobs that offer the opportunity for self-development. Industry conferences, mentorship programs, academic pursuits, internships, and skill advancement qualifications are best suited for you.

Famous 19s: Bill Clinton, Maria Sharapova, Benedict Cumberbatch, Gabrielle Bonheur "Coco" Chanel

- **(20)**

A typical 20 possesses self-awareness, tact, diplomacy, and is able to sense the feelings of others while effectively maintaining their center. Like birthday number 2, the 20s operate best as advisors and the power behind the throne. They are moved by harmony, beauty, and love. They are quite affectionate and desire lots of physical shows of affection, such as hugs, cuddles, etc. These individuals will give a southern belle a run for her money with their polite speech, impeccable manners, and regard for the time of others. But be careful; that same sugary tongue will deal out its special dose of poison when hurt.

Weaknesses

• There is a constant need for love, support, and encouragement, and failure to get this from a support system could lead to depression or a lack of determination.

• They are prone to extreme mood swings and a lack of self-esteem. They can be pleasant one minute and inconsolably sad the next.

Ideal Professions

They are suited to jobs where they act as advisors, ambassadors, or diplomats. They also shine in areas like medicine since they have the ability to deliver sensitive news with tact.

Famous 20s: Rihanna, Trevor Noah, Cindy Crawford, Ruby Rose

- (21)

The highly creative and imaginative 21 is a delight to be around. They have a strong desire to succeed, and for them, no mountain is too high. These social butterflies are highly influential and have a social calendar booked well in advance. They add an artistic flair to everything they do. They are always on the receiving end of affection and have opportunities to succeed thrown at them from every corner.

Weaknesses

• They have everything handed to them on a platter. As such, they can be quite materialistic and refuse to develop their talents, relying solely on charm and wit to get them through life.

• They are always a bundle of nervous energy due to their habit of overcommitting. Learning to say no will do them some good.

Ideal Professions

The ability to influence should not be wasted on small talk. It is necessary to channel focus towards jobs that require them to put ideas into words and charm the socks off people. Examples include sales, advertising, marketing, politics, writing, law, or philanthropy.

Famous 21s: Queen Elizabeth, Ernest Hemingway, Stephen King, Samuel L. Jackson.

• **(22)**

A great builder, organizer, and manager capable of materializing any dream they set their heart to, 22 is a picture-perfect example of patience, discipline, order, and more than an ample serving of intuition. Your pragmatism finds you front and center of large projects and at the helm of affairs. You are a walking paradox. You have tall and lofty dreams on the one hand, and on the other, you fear the height of your ambitions. This war between idealism and pragmatism is your defining characteristic.

Weaknesses

• They have a difficult time trusting anyone. As a result, they find it hard to delegate or be in a stable relationship.

• They spend a lot of time with friends who take advantage of them and have nothing to offer in return.

- An intense fear of failure that sometimes stops them from dreaming big.

Ideal Professions

It is easy for them to excel in any field they choose. Their blend of intuition, practicality, and diligence makes them adaptable to any job, from a hairstylist to a member of parliament.

Famous 22's: Naomi Campbell, Maggie Q, Meryl Streep, Arsène Wenger, Andrea Bocelli

- **(23)**

For a 23, life is an adventure, and because of this, they live every day as if it's their last. They are the chameleons of the group. A part of them craves change, while the other is flexible enough to adapt to whatever life throws at them. They are versatile, sociable, creative, sensitive, and, most of all, freedom-loving. Punishing a 23 is easy: just keep them cooped up in one spot for a considerable length of time. They are like smoke; their restless nerves will fray until they find a means to escape.

Weaknesses

- They have a penchant for thinking they are always right.

- They have a tendency to get bored and restless when they lack a positive outlet for their nervous energy.

- They like to overindulge in food, drugs, alcohol, and sex, quite possibly because of a fear of missing out on life.

Ideal Professions

Their discomfort with a routine makes them suitable for jobs with flexible hours that allow them to try new things. Pilots/flight attendants, travel bloggers, and even scientific researchers and inventors are good examples.

Famous 23s: Miley Cyrus, Ludovico Einaudi, Kangana Ragnaut, Alan Turing

- **(24)**

The self-sacrificing, sensible 24 is a hard worker who expects everyone to put in as much effort as they do. You have a gift for restoring peace and harmony to those around you, but your availability as a shoulder to cry on puts you in more trouble than you can handle. Your systematic approach to issues makes you easy to reason with but difficult to control. You are financially fortunate.

Weaknesses

- Overly emotional with a flair for melodrama, 24 tends to magnify issues concerning them. They have the woe-is-me act down to a science.

- People take advantage of your sensitive nature to ask for help; many times, you lose yourself in a bid to satisfy others.

- Their intuitive nature makes them impractical, and as such, they need constant advice from rational people.

Ideal Professions

It is essential for 24s to pursue a career not for financial benefit but for the purpose of self-realization and inner peace. They are attracted to teaching, art, medicine, social work.

Famous 24s: Steve Jobs, Floyd Mayweather, Jean-Paul Gaultier, Bob Dylan

- **(25)**

The 25s have a sound rational mind with the ability to think intellectually and analytically. They believe in the motto, "for every problem, there is a solution." You are able to investigate and thoroughly research subjects to discover information. You require solitude and tranquility to recharge your batteries.

Weaknesses

• Prone to mood swings and addictions,

• Most of them usually have backgrounds with bitter childhood memories. As a result, they are cynical and mistrustful of the intentions of others.

Ideal Professions

Their ability to investigate and research makes them suitable for jobs in law and law enforcement, healthcare, academia, history, etc.

Famous 25s: Virginia Woolf, Ralph Waldo Emerson, George Orwell, Aretha Franklin, Pablo Picasso.

- **(26)**

26 is great with money and talented in the business. No one under 26 is ashamed to accept responsibility. They are proud of their accomplishments. They are realists who see the bigger picture but neglect the fine print. It is a challenge for them to balance their love of materialism with their need to help others. They love being surrounded by harmonious company but have trouble making friends as they find it hard to relate to people their age.

Weaknesses

• A dog-eat-dog attitude in business makes you inconsiderate towards others.

• Difficulty in accepting mistakes and failure in life turns you into a pessimist.

• Having an ostentatious attitude, your need for social status and acceptance makes you spend a little too lavishly.

Ideal Professions

You thrive in vocations where you are given the opportunity to be proud of your accomplishments, or else you might lose interest. Business, sports, finance, and commerce. Your tendency to lead a team makes you an excellent team leader or manager.

Famous 26s: Jose Mourinho, Ellen DeGeneres, Melania Trump, DJ Khaled.

- **(27)**

Guiding others comes naturally to you because of your gift of insight and understanding. While others think within certain conventions, you don't just think outside the box; to you, there is no box! For this reason, you are tolerant of the viewpoints of others and value the right to express yourself freely. You have an aristocratic bearing and are a true humanitarian whose satisfaction comes from the act of helping others. The influence of 2 and 7 makes you fiercely independent, with a desire for a spiritual connection.

Weaknesses

- They are late bloomers. They need a lot of time to choose their path.
- Impatience and impulsiveness expose them to self-destructive behavior.

Ideal Professions

Any field that is in line with art and creativity is fine. They are also excellent leaders, managers, and executives in the fields of religion, politics, and law.

Famous 27s: Wolfgang Amadeus Mozart, Henry Kissinger, Quentin Tarantino, Ulysses Grant

- (28)

Your gift for leadership is best expressed through teamwork. Unlike many who are given to loud and brash displays of power, you apply rationality and gentle coercion. Your ambition and independence mean you are always jumping headfirst into taking risks, which usually pay off handsomely. You are unapologetically yourself and do not mind standing out in a crowd.

Weaknesses

- Fond of their own thought process and deeply averse to change.

- They can be temperamental, jealous, and competitive when they are not successful, complimented for their efforts, or not the center of attention.

- They make money easily and spend it the same way.

- They may appear aloof because they have a hard time trusting anyone.

Ideal Professions

You are so versatile and have a variety of career options. Since it is rare for you to run out of ideas, you will thrive in jobs in commerce, tourism, politics, consumer goods, advertising, entertainment, and event management.

Famous 28s: Lady Gaga, Elon Musk, Jacqueline Kennedy Onassis, Bill Gates.

- (29)

The highly intuitive mind of 29 thinks in Technicolor. You pull ideas from the sky like magicians pull bunnies from a hat. You feel a connection to all things spiritual and have a strong dependence on your environment. As a leader, you are idealistic and philosophical, though, like Luna Lovegood, your detachment from the world does not mean you are incapable of conducting yourself in social situations. If patience were a currency, you would be the richest of all the numbers.

Weaknesses

- You are a late bloomer, which is why, in your youth, you are given to bouts of mood swings, unnecessary drama, and fights.
- They are very unpredictable and can be extremely jealous of others.

Ideal Professions

Your idealism makes you slightly unsuitable for the cutthroat world of business, but it is possible to find a person who thrives in the oddest of professions since they generally go for professions that emulate their natural talents.

Famous 29s: Oprah Winfrey, Michael Jackson, Chadwick Boseman, John F. Kennedy

- **(30)**

Your high level of creativity makes you an artist at heart. It is advisable that if you do not have an artistic career, you should consider taking it up as something to pass the time. Your quick wit, charismatic nature, and communication skills attract people to you in droves. People forgive you for things they would never pardon anyone else for. In return, you bless them with your presence and your special brand of feel-good energy.

Weaknesses

- They have people around them all the time but find it hard to create and maintain meaningful relationships.

• Their childlike innocence and naiveté can be frustrating. For those they are in a relationship with, it's like dating Peter Pan.

Ideal Professions

Any field with creative and artistic endeavors will suit them like a glove. They can write, paint, perform on strange occasions, do voice acting, and a myriad of other things.

Famous 30's: Tiger Woods, Piers Morgan, Cameron Diaz, Vincent Van Gogh.

- **(31)**

A lover of traditional values, community, and family, you favor practicality and perform your duties with precision and diligence. You are a nature lover, brimming with creativity and artistic talent that seeks ways of concrete expression. All in all, you are a harmonious blend of function, form, and aesthetics.

Organization and leadership come naturally to you. Your well-honed senses miss nothing. This is why you are the fine-tooth comb in any field you apply yourself to. You are ten times more prepared than others for surprise eventualities. You do not suffer foolery well, but your magnetism seems to attract it. People rely on you at work, but you still feel you have not found your calling in life.

Weaknesses

• Set in their traditional ways, they are hardly receptive to new ideas.

• The tendency to overwork – leading to frustration.

• They have difficulty trusting people.

Ideal Professions

Your talents are versatile, and you are suited to any profession. However, since you are an excellent leader and a skilled diplomat, you shine in fields requiring that you act in a managerial or leadership capacity.

Famous 31s: Baba Vanga, Justin Timberlake, J.K. Rowling, Al Gore.

Chapter 8: Life Path Number

The life path number is one of your numerology chart's most important core numbers. Alternative names for life path numbers include your birth force number, ruling number, or birth path number. Your life path number is the first number any numerologist will analyze as it reveals:

- Your Personality (who you are).

- Your Life's Mission (the reason behind your existence on Earth and lessons you will master while accomplishing your mission).

The life path number not only outlines your inherent strengths and weaknesses as a person but foretells the kind of experiences that may come your way as you fulfill your purpose on Earth.

Calculating Life Path Numbers

The life path number is calculated using the date of birth. It is calculated in three ways:

- Reducing down
- Adding across
- Adding down

Of the three methods of calculation, numerologists deem the first two to be the most accurate. Neither method is "better" than the other. They are used by practitioners as a simple matter of personal preference or for ease of calculation. Feel free to use whichever method appeals to you. The general guideline, regardless of which method you choose, is to reduce double-digit numbers to a single-digit number unless the total figure falls into the master number category (11, 22, or 33).

The Reducing-Down Method

Step 1: Add up the numbers in the day, month, and year of your birth date individually.

Step 2: Reduce double digits in any of the summations (if any) to single-digit numbers.

Step 3: add all the derived numbers and reduce them to a single digit. If the total yields a master number, leave it as it is.

Note that some numerologists are of the opinion that master numbers should be further reduced to single digits in life path calculations while others object to it. The choice of calculation is up to you. For numerologists in the latter category, this method is the most accurate to determine master numbers. Let's find the life path for the birth date of January 3, 1906.

Month = 1

Day = 3

Year = 1906

1+9+0+6=16; 1+6= 7

Total: 1+3+7= 11

The life path number for the above date of birth is 11/2, a master number.

The Adding-Across Method

This is the second and simplest method of all.

Step 1: Add a plus sign after each individual number in your birthdate and add each digit across the board. Ensure you write down the full birth year as it appears on your birth certificate. For instance, if you were born in the year 1960, calculate it as 1960, not 60.

Step 2: Sum up all double-digit numbers where applicable and reduce the digits until you derive a single-digit number. The exceptions to this case are totals like 11, which becomes 11/2, 22 becomes 22/4, and 33 becomes 33/6

Let's calculate the life path number for the date January 3, 1906

Month + Day + Year

1 + 3 + 1 + 9 + 0 + 6= 20;

(Further reduction) 2+0= 2

As you can see from the example above, steps are taken to further reduce the double-digit result to get a single-digit life path number.

When looking at compound totals, it pays to take note of the number 0 in totals like 10, 20, 30, and so on before reducing them down. This is because the number 0 is not just a placeholder or a null digit. It represents spirit, wholeness, inclusivity, and the infinite possibilities offered by the universe. In numerology, 0 is thought to embody the power of God, which is why it acts like a chameleon, amplifying the vibration of the number that exists beside it.

So, if we apply this logic in calculating the life path number for January 3, 1906= 20; 2+0= 1 (life path number 2 amplified by 0).

In some cases, you may end up with a single-digit life path number that needs no further reduction. Here's an example:

March 2, 2001: 3+2+2+0+0+1= 8

Chaldean numerology places great importance on the value known as the compound total. The benefit of using the second method over the first, apart from the ease of calculation, is that the double-digit total (compound number) post summation provides extra knowledge about the type of life path number it is.

For instance, a 14/5 life path number will differ from that of a 23/5. This is because the former contains the number vibrations 1 and 4 while the latter has 2 and 3. They may have similar reduced single digits, but their expressions will differ slightly. Thus, an insight into the compound total helps you understand better your life path expression.

From the two methods of calculation described above, you have observed that one calculation favors the revelation of a master number over the other.

Adding-Down Method

This is the third and least commonly used method of calculating life path numbers.

Step 1: Sum up the Month, Day, and Year in a single column. So, for October 13, 1969:

10

+ 13

1969

————

Total 1992

You could decide to reduce the year of birth down to two digits, so for instance, 1969 becomes (1+9+6+9=25). In this example, I am choosing to leave the year of birth as is.

Step 2: Sum up the digits in the total and reduce them to a single digit for the life path number. Remember, the exceptions are the master numbers 11/2, 22/4, and 33/6. So, the life path number for the birth date in our previous example is worked out like this:

10

+ 13

1969

————

Total 1992

1 + 9 + 9 + 2 = 21

2 + 1 = 3

The life path number is 3.

Now, let's repeat the adding down method for the date January 3, 1906

1
+ 3
1906

Total 1910
1 + 9 + 1 + 0 = 11

From the three different methods discussed, it is obvious to see the reducing down and adding down method gave a master number for the same date while the adding across method gave a single-digit figure amplified by 0. Which calculation is accurate? That's the conundrum! Since neither method is accurate or inaccurate, just different, the method you use depends on your personal taste, and the methods will likely affect the answers you obtain.

Numerology is not a one size fits all jumper. Note, however, that only the master number calculations produce this challenge. This difference in answers could occur anytime you end up with either a 2, 4, or 6. For this reason, many numerologists use all three methods and go with the majority rule figure for their answer. The best option is understanding the traits of the master numbers and comparing them to their corresponding single numbers to determine which of them is the best fit.

Descriptions of Each Life Path Number

Life Path Number 1 — The Individualistic Leader

Life path 1 individuals are pioneers who created a cut above the rest to continually break away from the mold and walk by their own rules. Your courage, creativity, positive nature, and tenacity are your greatest strengths. Your uniqueness sometimes makes you feel different and alienated from the rest of the crowd. Don't be disheartened. Your DNA is fashioned to stand out, not fit in.

Your individuality is your gift to the universe, so use it to your advantage and, instead of trying to let societal rules and norms get to you, take steps to improve the quality of your own life. Dare to believe in yourself but be careful not to let your ambitious nature get the better of you because there is no such thing as competition on this plane in the grand scheme of things.

When you begin to understand and accept the interconnectedness of all things, only then will you reach your full potential. Surround yourself with individuals who believe in your dream because your life purpose is only fulfilled when you guide others lovingly toward causes that benefit humanity.

Affirmation: *"I choose to walk a path that helps me embrace my independence, strength, and individuality."*

Life Path Number 2 – The Collaborator and Peacemaker

A sense of harmony and unity is a major requirement for people with life path 2. Tuning in to their emotions and that of others comes naturally to them. You are honest to a fault, a terrific listener and counselor with the uncanny ability to get people to tell you their deepest darkest fears and secrets.

You possess the gift of both energetic and verbal healing. You cannot tolerate disagreements, and you always leave good impressions on the people you meet. You are dedicated to nurturing relationships and give the shirt off your back to help someone in need.

Live by your personal values even when it means you may be criticized and underappreciated. Never forget to stand up for yourself when it counts and ask for help when the pressure from helping others makes you feel like you might crack. It is okay to accept help too. You are fulfilling your life purpose when you care for, heal and nurture others as long as you do not sacrifice your needs and independence in the process.

Affirmation: "*My sensitivity is my gift to the world. I love, heal and care for myself and others.*"

Life Path Number 3 — The Expressive Creative

A life path 3 individual is magnetic, creative, and expressive. Their communicative abilities shine, whether it is among friends, colleagues, or anyone else. Eternally optimistic, they radiate boundless positivity, imagination, and humor that help them in their quest to succeed. Putting their talents to good use helps improve their well-being emotionally, physically, and mentally.

Though one of their weaknesses is commitment (to things, tasks, and people), they speak honestly from their hearts and are always willing to lift or inspire people. People envy their personality, intelligence, and how easy their life seems on the outside, but life path 3 struggles within to balance their lofty ideals with realism. Their ability to express has a darker side seen in the act of gossiping, criticizing, exaggerating, and complaining. Once they understand the power in their words, they will realize how they sabotage themselves with negative speech.

Affirmation: "*I am a center for love, joy, and positive energy. I express my thoughts to create a happy life.*"

Life Path Number 4 — The Diligent Worker

Practicality, reliability, logic, a keen mind, and strong will are some of the traits ascribed to individuals with life path 4. They know exactly what they want and are not afraid to work long and hard to achieve it. They have organized balanced lives and are the pillars of any community or endeavor they find themselves in. Their tenacity and discipline get the work done, but their greatest struggle is doing away with their fixed mindset and opinions about certain things.

If 4 had a quote, it would definitely be, *"If it ain't broke, don't fix it."* Dynamism and thinking on their feet are not their forte, which is why they miss out on a lot of opportunities since they waste a lot of precious time thinking about it. But, when they apply themselves to an idea, no matter how new it is, they always excel.

As a life path 4 person, you fulfill your life's mission when you uplift others by using practical step-by-step solutions to their problems. Do this in such a way that you do not demand perfection from yourself and others. Find time to relax and let your hair down.

Affirmation: *"I let go of my need to control; I seek to promote order that makes the world a better place."*

Life Path Number 5 — The Free-Spirited Adventurer

Individuals with a life path number of 5 are the most prejudice-free people on the planet. They are always ready with out-of-the-box thinking and solutions to problems. The motto "You Only Live Once" is more than a cool saying; for them, it is a way of life. For this reason, they seem unbothered about what the future may bring, not because they are unafraid, but because they have what it takes to adapt.

Their self-indulgence and focus on the present lead them to make some very damaging decisions financially, romantically, and otherwise. But they bounce back quickly. They have a variety of talents but are advised to use both their talents and freedom wisely. Their life purpose is fulfilled when they teach others what they have learned through experience.

Affirmation: *"I embrace myself for who, and what I represent. I am willing to explore every life experience to become a better version of myself."*

Life Path Number 6 — The Responsible Caretaker

Ever heard Immanuel Kant saying, "veni, vidi, amavi?" It is an Italian saying outlining rules for happiness as "something to do, someone to love and something to hope for." This is the golden rule adhered to by life path 6.

Blessed with enough compassion to feed a small community, the 6s spread light, love, and generosity wherever they go. They are happiest when in close contact with others, nurturing and caring for them. They dream of having their own family or a domestic setting because being responsible for others brings them joy.

Their need to cater to others and put themselves in the shoes of anyone else but their own ensures they are burdened with a myriad of responsibilities which they juggle really well. There is a dark side to caring for others. It can be draining, and there are many occasions where your love is neither appreciated nor reciprocated. And while you are blessed with a lot of "love reserve," you must seek a balance between caring for yourself and others. As a 6, you are fulfilling your purpose by tapping into your selflessness and providing unconditional love to all and sundry, without ignoring your own needs in the process.

Affirmation: *"I am compassionate with others and myself; I am grateful for my life and its lessons."*

Life Path Number 7 — The Contemplative Truth Seeker

Life path 7 individuals radiate peace, love, and serene energy. These deep thinkers question the reason behind everything and seek to understand the mysteries of the universe. 7s as seekers of knowledge are drawn to spirituality, and even if they are not spiritual, life always throws them an experience that forces them to open their minds.

These individuals are usually introverted, aloof, withdrawn, and feel lonely or left out at times despite their intense need to relate well with others. The only exceptions to this pattern of social ineptitude are for those with an "outgoing" astrology chart (containing core numbers of either 1, 3, or 5) or those with a life path of 24/7.

6 has the potential to succeed in any career because of their love for research and the extrapolation of information; however, they may gravitate towards careers in history, spirituality, or metaphysics. 7s are fulfilling their purpose when they uncover the truth and discover the hidden meaning behind life and existence.

Affirmation: *"I am deeply connected to my higher self. I am blessed with the gifts to discover spirituality that benefits humanity."*

Life Path Number 8 — The Business Minded Executive

With life path number 8, rest assured that the universe has granted you wealth, prosperity, and power. These confident, practical, and gifted leaders live by their own principles and exude an air of abundance. Blessed with the ability of manifestation, their powerful minds choose to focus on their hopes and dreams rather than on their fears or uncertainties.

They are great judges of character with excellence in business and politics, but their workaholic tendencies and propensity to focus on materialism over everything else are two of their greatest weaknesses. Success to you is directly proportional to status, achievement, and money. This belief puts other aspects of your life, such as your romantic life, family, and social life, in jeopardy. Your life path is fulfilled when you are empowered, have a healthier relationship with money, and are generous to the people around you.

Affirmation: *"I am a success magnet, I attract abundance, and I am in control of my destiny."*

Life Path Number 9 — The Empathetic Humanitarian

Philanthropy and the spirit of compassion are first and foremost in the heart and minds of individuals with life paths 9. Regardless of their fields of endeavor (which are many), they know they exist to make the world a better place for others to live in.

Their challenge, however, is their judgment and bias towards others and a failure to accept their own imperfections. Facing this challenge is the first step to making a change in an already imperfect world. Their creative and artistic side is drawn to art, nature, beauty, harmony, design, public speaking, or any other field, which gives their imagination and creativity an outlet to shine.

9s, like the 7s, are attracted to mysticism and spirituality. Some even have extrasensory perception. Many 9s have either had a hard time growing up or have been subject to family drama over the years. Being able to see a silver lining in negativity and being able to forgive yourself and others are two of the ways that you can remain selfless enough to fulfill your purpose of spreading kindness and love to humanity.

Affirmation: *"I release the hurt from the past to embrace the present; I care for others and receive care in return."*

Life Path Number 11 — The Inspiring Teacher

Life path 11 is one of the master numbers in numerology. As a result, individuals with this life path are blessed with an increased level of intuition, insight, and spiritual awareness. This life path is always a bit of a challenge because of the opposing forces of 1 and 2. This implies that the independent, take-charge attitude of 1 could be influenced by the emotional sensitivity of 2.

Your purpose in life is to discover your truth and achieve self-mastery. It is also essential to let go of your ego so that you can truly love and believe in yourself. Your ability to feel intensely and uplift others must be balanced by the ability to set clear boundaries and knowing when to say no, serving humanity without letting yourself go in the process. Once you step into your power and surrender to a cause greater than yourself, there will be no limit to what you can do, be or achieve. Your purpose as an 11/2 life path is to work for the greater good to make a real impact in the world.

Affirmation: *"I inspire, enable and empower others to conceive an extraordinary life."*

Life Path Number 22 — The Master Builder

Numerologists claim that this is the most powerful yet most challenging life path number of all. As a 22, you are a powerhouse of optimism and positivity who has the ability to manifest dreams into reality through practical methods. Your rational and methodical approach makes you a gifted manager, organizer, and all-around "people-person." You are a visionary with the ability to see the bigger picture without missing the tiny details. You sometimes suffer an inferiority complex, refusing help due to fear of criticism or shame.

You have mastered appearing controlled on the surface, but like the proverbial duck, you are flapping around, overflowing with emotions beneath. An overbearing attitude and constant self-censure are maladaptive behaviors that can stop you from reaching the heights you desire for yourself.

It is your responsibility to evolve so that you transform your archetype into one that is grounded and centered at all times. Once you can achieve this, the universe will constantly have your back as long as it is for a cause that benefits humanity. Your life purpose is fulfilled when you create, expand, and promote causes greater than your personal interests.

Affirmation: *"I exist to serve humanity with everything I possess in a way that improves my own life in turn."*

Life Path Number 33 — The Cosmic Guardian

A life path number 33/6 means you exist to bring happiness and joy to the world and to others through your powers of compassion, creativity, and talent for healing. Your nurturing abilities make you gifted with people, especially children. The zesty vibrations of the fun-loving 3 are manifested in your child-like innocence and how you see the world as something of perpetual wonder.

Do not forget that no one can draw from an empty well. While giving love to others, do not hesitate to keep some for yourself. Do not force care on others to the extent that you interfere with their free will. Allow people to take charge of their own lives and heal sometimes. This is where you apply logic to ensure control of your emotions. You are fulfilling your purpose when you apply yourself to healing the world through compassion, creative expression, teaching, or healing.

Affirmation: *"I fully embrace my divine calling to heal, love, and teach humanity."*

Chapter 9: Your Growth Number

What Are Growth Numbers?

The growth number is also called the *key number*, and it is a number based on the summation value of the vibrations inherent in the individual letters of your first (documented) birth name. The sum is reduced to a single digit or a master number. The growth number describes the energy which enlightens your life experience. It permits you to have a clearer understanding of the lessons you are here on earth to learn. This is why, even though the growth number is not a core number, it is considered a sub-lesson to the life path number, which is a core number in numerology.

The growth number points to inherent latent traits you (or your little one) can encourage or develop. Even though the growth number is not a core number, it is connected to each of the core numbers in a special way. For instance, since the growth number is derived from the given first name, it is included in the calculation of the soul urge and destiny numbers. This means that whatever name you choose for yourself (or your child) has a 50 percent effect on the core numbers.

Karmic lessons are derived from the summation of the first name (growth number), middle, and last name. The maturity number is derived from the addition of the destiny and life path numbers. Hence, the growth number is 50 percent of your destiny number, seeing as it is calculated from your documented first name. This shows that even more than what you eat, you *are* what name you are known as. It is not an overstatement to say that the name you choose determines a lot of things about your existence.

Calculating Growth Numbers

Growth numbers are calculated using the Pythagorean chart. For instance, let's calculate the growing number of the name Cedric Adams White.

C – 3
E – 5
D – 4
R – 9
I – 9
C – 3

3 + 5 + 4 + 9 + 9 + 3 = 33 (No further reduction is needed since it is a master number).

Some names could have a single-digit growth number, like the name Jane.

J – 1
A – 1
N – 5
E – 5
1 + 1 + 5 + 5 = 12
1 + 2 = 3

Some Facts to Note about Growth Numbers

Growth numbers are general and not specific in the description. The extent and manner in which your growth number affects you are dependent on many variables, namely your core numbers, interests, etc.

Subtle differences in the spelling of the name can affect the growth number. For instance, the name Anne has a growing number of 16 (1+6) = 7. Note the karmic debt number 16, which revolves around issues concerning trust. Another variant of the same name, ANN, is 1+5+5=11/2. Note the master number present.

Master numbers are never reduced to growing numbers. This is because it is necessary to acknowledge the intense vibrations they contain. Think of your growth number as a bonus gift. Because it is the only aspect of the numerology chart that exclusively yields the positive expression of a number, it can redress the balance of debts, potential weaknesses, conflicts, and so on in other areas of the chart.

For instance, if you were born on a day that gives the 4 (13) life path number, meaning it carries the karmic debt of selfishness, neglect, and laziness in a past life, taking on a name with the growing number of 1 will help smooth out the potential hardships specific to the 1 energy. The extra 1 gives an added vibrational boost that helps you combat laziness. This aspect of balance and counterbalance should be handled by an expert numerologist during a consultation so that a list of suitable names can be drawn out, and the one that gives you the most benefit can be chosen.

It is worth bearing in mind that each growth number has both positive and negative aspects. For this reason, there is a need to cultivate the positive habits of our numbers so that you encounter less resistance in your existence on earth.

1 — Love, Light, Creator, Leader

Balanced: An extremely creative soul with the power to manifest their dreams into reality. You are independent, confident, original, and a goal-getter. They crave perfection and excellence in all their endeavors. All in all, this vibration is a recipe for entrepreneurs, innovators, and pioneers. And the law of attraction surrounds you in all its glory.

Unbalanced: Aggressive, unfocused, little or no power of manifestation, tyrannical, and overconfident. They over-analyze the present, past, and future and lack manifesting abilities. As a result, relationships, projects, and other endeavors fall apart for no apparent reason. Your social circle is lacking because of your negative and domineering attitude.

Note: This growth number will be thoroughly amplified or influenced by other names on the chart.

2 — Diplomat, Harmony Bringer

Balanced: Diplomacy runs in their blood. They are successful mediators and peacekeepers. They work best with a team because group settings and harmonious cooperation are their forte. They are sensitive, intuitive, and empathize with others seamlessly. They are adaptable, flexible, and comfortable in the shadows; their qualities are more mental than physical as they are not as physically strong as 1s.

Unbalanced: Issues with self-confidence, fear, indecision, being submissive to a fault, fears of being alone, extremely sensitive, and prone to depression or mood swings. They can be pessimistic when things do not go according to plan.

3 — Creative, Vibrant, Expressive

Balanced: 3 has a way with words, and their skills as master communicators allow them to express themselves creatively (particularly with oration or writing). For them, it's always glass half full. They have an unending zest for life and living. They make the best salespeople, comedians, motivational speakers, and entertainers.

Unbalanced: Irresponsibility, overconfidence, indifference to the plight of others but themselves, exaggeration, penchant for melodrama (most of which they are responsible for starting), liars, the deep-seated fear of failure concerning their talents. They are often unable to sustain long-term relationships (romantic or not), oversensitivity to criticism, and immaturity.

4 — Reliable, Stable, Practical

Balanced: Principled, foundation builder, innovator, closet rebel. Their genius births a lot of ideas that need a creative outlet to be made manifest. They are aware of their duties and what it takes to achieve them. These perfectionists are at the top of the chain when it comes to organizational abilities and getting things done in the most practical way. Consistency, diligence, routine, and structure are their watchwords. They have hidden (sometimes dormant) abilities for spiritual healing and light work. They are family-oriented and function better when the home front is at peace.

Unbalanced: Stickler for routine, which leads to a rigid mindset, miserly nature, pessimism about life, obsession with details to the point of perfectionism. They often harbor distrust in what the future holds. They exhibit fear of missing out (FOMO) and, ironically, are also afraid of what tomorrow may bring.

5 — Ingenious, Adventurous, Optimistic

Balanced: Artful, enthusiastic, imaginative, and adaptable to change with the times, 5 has a magnetism that they wear like a second skin. They are outgoing, exuberant, and "explorers" in numerology. They have versatile talents and find they excel at almost anything they try. Great at all forms of communication, 5 is a charmer, a social butterfly, and an all-around entertainer. 5 is unable to sit still. Their gifts, when channeled positively, could do wonders for their careers and finances.

Unbalanced: Fickle-minded and extremely unreliable, they can either be passionate and driven or be nonchalant and dependent on others. They are always in a financial pickle because of their bad investments and spending habits, temperamental, easily and endlessly distracted, and prone to addiction and overindulgence.

6 — Nurturing, Loving, Loyal

Balanced: Because of their relationship to the planet Venus, number 6 is primarily focused on domestic life and relationships. They are magnetic, artistic, and devoted to their friends and loved ones. They are level-headed and adaptable and have an innate desire to bring peace and harmony to everyone in their environment. For this reason, they tend to nurture people at the expense of their own happiness and comfort, attracting endless responsibilities they really don't need. Many express a secret love for mystic sciences such as tantra, witchcraft, the occult, etc.

Unbalanced: Irritatingly self-righteous, narrow-minded with traditional beliefs, hypocritical, prone to envy, burnout, melancholy, and temper flare-ups.

7 — Spiritual, Wise, Analytical

Balanced: According to Pythagoras, the father of numerology, the number 7 is shaped like a shepherd's hook, and it symbolizes the path of kundalini energy from the base of the spine to the third eye (tisra til/tenth gate) on our forehead between our eyebrows. As a highly spiritual number, individuals with a growing number of 7 are innovators and visionaries. They are resilient, strong, with sharp minds, especially in matters relating to spirit and spirituality. They are always researching and constantly try to decipher information. Reclusive, private, introverted, and indifferent to the mundane, they are driven to understand the hidden mysteries of the human mind and cosmos. They have problems with social connections, friends, and relationships.

Unbalanced: Emotionally distant, fearing failure, domineering attitude, inability to empathize, difficulty in expressing emotions, suffering from crippling anxiety, temperamental pessimism, over-critical of themselves and others, prone to depression and loneliness.

8 — Logical, Ambitious, Tenacious

Balanced: Their sound and rational judgment makes them fantastic leaders and executives. They are goal-oriented, assertive, resourceful, and highly focused. For this reason, they tend to gravitate toward positions of authority in their chosen field to become self-established business owners. Their charisma and tenacity often influence them to take on challenges that seem greater than they are. Often, in their bid to "make their mark" on the world, they concentrate on financial and material pursuits at the expense of their family and relationships. This is why they have problems balancing their professional and personal lives.

Unbalanced: Materialistic, self-serving, a desire to control people or situations, domineering, temperamental, mistrustful of others, tactless, obsessive, anti-social

9 — Mystic, Humanitarian, Teacher

Balanced: The number 9 is a firm believer in the adage "kindness costs nothing." The true humanitarians of the numerology chart thrive on change, transformation, and goodwill. They see the bigger picture in all things.

Their nature demands that they "fix" the world's imperfections, which is totally impossible. Their need for harmony is balanced out by their desire to delve into spirituality and the unknown. 9. They could either be in touch with their instinct and elemental magnetism, or they could be oblivious to their instinctual power so that it becomes stagnant. The typical response of a 9 to painful situations is denial or an attempt to live in a false construct of bliss and peace. The greatest challenge a 9 has is the need to overcome their indecisiveness and negative thoughts.

Unbalanced: Disconnected from reality, unforgiving, fault-finding, chronic worriers, conceited, difficulty in trusting others, frustrated with mundane events.

11 — Goal-getter, Spiritual, Philanthropist

Balanced: Rational, adaptable, and creative enough to make a difference in the world, the number 11 is a master number that has similar traits to the number 2. They are empathetic individuals who really mean it when they say they know how others feel. They are charismatic with extensive knowledge of hidden truths. 11 has an underlying sense of justice and fairness, and their methods are unconventional.

Unbalanced: Caring about the opinions of others, obstinate, egotistic, prone to temper tantrums and mood swings.

22 — Ambitious, Cooperative, Humanitarian

Balanced: Capable of manifestation through cooperation and relationships. They are dedicated to connecting with others towards a common goal. Their purpose in life is to be of service to others and to humanity. 22 has a knack for integrating their knowledge of metaphysics into day-to-day living. They have no patience for fools or pretenders. Their life experience is riddled with hardships that point them in the direction of self-fulfillment in service. Many 22s have chosen to reincarnate for the purpose of helping humanity (case in point, the Dalai Lama). They are drawn to the universal language of music.

Unbalanced: Moody, aimless, angry, aloof, impractical, big talkers.

33 — Broad-minded, Selfless, Motivators/Guardians

Balanced: Knowledgeable, zealous, with a powerful need to help others even when they do not feel at their best, 33 has mastered the art of selfless service. 33s are usually slow bloomers and do not awaken their talents until maturity or middle age. Sensitive, responsible, and cautious, 33 is known as the master guardian or teacher.

Their purpose in life is to teach and provide guidance to others using their life experiences. They are specialists in motivating people and raising their vibrations. This is why they end up leaving a legacy of positive footprints in the world. Mastering the vibrations of this number is quite challenging, and to see one who has embraced in totality their gifts as a master teacher is indeed rare.

Unbalanced: Perfectionists, self-righteous, controlling, compulsive liars (because they fear hurting the feelings of others), careless, burdened by the gift of extreme insight, low self-esteem.

General Questions Concerning Growth and Name Number Calculators

Q: Is it compulsory to calculate the name numbers for documented names I seldom or never use in real life?

A: Absolutely. Your documented or legal name has vibrations influencing every sphere of your life. Even in situations where you use a shortened version of your first name, your middle name, or even an alias, the influence of your given name cannot be ignored or denied. The only way to get an accurate numerology reading is to use your full name as it appears on your birth certificate, whether you frequently use it or not.

Q: What about instances where names have changed following matrimony, anglicization, or divorce?

A: Your documented name is still the major name you are influenced by regardless of whatever life experiences you may have had that warranted a compulsory name change or amendment.

Q: What about a case where a name has certain letters or accents that are not in the Pythagorean chart?

A: If your given name has letters or accents like å, â, é, è, ç, ï, ñ or ø, it is advised that you use the numeric value of the letter as it appears in the Pythagorean chart without the accent. For compound letters like the "Æ" commonly found in the Scandinavian, Norwegian, or Icelandic alphabet, you have to split the letters "into individual constituents "a" and "e." In which case, a = 1, and e = 5, the summation of which has the numerical value of 6.

Q: Is it possible to change my name vibration by choosing a new name for myself?

A: The answer is a big no. The systems that keep track of name vibrations on this plane are replicated in the etheric plane, where the akashic records are kept. These records contain an energetic signature of everything that has transpired on this earthly plane and to mankind in all times, whether past, present, or future. The akashic records can only be accessed, read, and their contents cleared or changed by an experienced numerologist or practitioner. Employing the help of an expert numerologist for a name change remains the only way to rewrite a name in these records, which inadvertently changes the experience you attract on a physical and spiritual level.

Chapter 10: Your Destiny Number

The Meaning and Importance of Destiny Numbers

In Pythagorean or Western numerology, the destiny number is the second most important number in an individual's numerology chart. Alternative names for the destiny number include name number, expression number, and complete name number. Chaldean numerologists refer to the destiny number as the purpose number.

The name might differ between both systems, but the common theme is the fact that both systems acknowledge the destiny number, which reveals your life's mission and the feats you are destined to accomplish on earth. Many practitioners believe that destiny numbers should be considered along with the life path number when making career choices. This is because the destiny number reveals tasks or jobs you will be successful in handling as well as the aspects of your life (personality traits, goals, stumbling blocks) that must be refined to help you reach your full potential.

The destiny number is calculated from your original, documented name, as it is written on your birth certificate. Whether or not you use or like those names, they reveal the predetermined destiny you were born to fulfill. This applies to circumstances where you have changed your name for one reason or another or taken on an extra name following marriage, adoption, or religious rites. No matter what the circumstance, the energy from your given name remains with you for the rest of your mortal existence.

If the circumstances were such that your parents couldn't decide on a name for you for a while and the name "baby" was written on your birth certificate for a time period as brief as one hour, then the name "baby" must be considered during the numerological reading. If you were adopted and are unaware of your birth name, then your adopted name may be read instead, always bearing in mind that an essential piece of information will be lacking from your reading.

Western numerologists are of the opinion that a name change or an alias based on your birth name yields a new destiny number, but this new number does not in any way, shape or form affect your original destiny number vibration. Instead, it works alongside it, boosting its power and adding that extra oomph to your life in the form of additional lessons, life experiences, abilities, and talents.

The destiny number shows how you react to situations you encounter in life. Are you someone that prefers the spotlight, or are you content with a supportive role? Do you wade through life as an active or passive participant? This number also shows how well you work and relate to others. This number is a melting pot of both your inner persona and the persona you want the rest of the world to see.

What Name to Use in Destiny Number Calculation

To get the most accurate figure for your destiny or expression number, it is advised that you use your name as it appears on your birth registration, birth certificate, or whichever legally recognized document records the name you received at the time of your birth, even if you rarely use it, or are not well known by those names.

This also means that if your name is misspelled or your mother's maiden name is on record, it will be included with a hyphen after your surname. Alternately, if you were given the name "baby girl" or "baby boy," these names must be taken into consideration. There are other special circumstances that may arise, such as:

- **The addition of an extra name post-birth**: Some cultures and religious rites insist on an additional name. For instance, the Catholic rites of baptism and confirmation require the adoption of the name of a saint. Or maybe Uncle Giles' condition for inheriting his estate was that you took his name. As much as you may want that inheritance, your new moniker isn't the name you would use when calculating your destiny number. You are advised to revert to your birth name.

- **Missing or lost birth certificate**: It is possible that your birth certificate may have been missing, or lost due to a fire incident, flood, or a lazy midwife who neglected to report your fabulous arrival into the world. There is an easy fix for this problem. You could order your birth certificates from the registrar in the state or county of your birth, the chief of vital statistics in the United States, or similar offices in developed nations. Simply search the internet for a suitable office and voila! Problem solved. If none of the solutions work, you could use the name that was listed on your school documents as an infant.

• **Adoption:** It is normal practice to have adoption records sealed in many countries. This makes it difficult for adopted children to obtain their original birth certificates. If this is the case for you, you could search the internet for organizations that specialize in the research of adoption records. If this is impossible, then, and only then, can you use the name given by your adoptive parents. The fun fact about adoptive names is that when adoptees are finally able to retrieve their original birth certificate, they discover that the destiny numbers derived from their given names are similar to those calculated from their adoptive names.

• **Birth in foreign countries:** If your parents were living in a country like North Korea, Japan, or the middle east, you may discover that in place of your birth name is hangul, kanji, or Arabic calligraphy, then do not fret. Use the name your parents intended for you to have or your full name as a child.

• **Suffixes like I, II-IV, or Junior:** If there is a generational suffix such as a roman numeral or "Junior" attached to your name, numerologists advise that you use your given name without the additional bells and whistles in order to arrive at the most accurate calculation of your destiny number. This is because the suffixes are not an essential part of your name but are merely add-on references.

• **Name change following marriage or a legal procedure:** Some people may have had to change their names after marriage or as part of a witness protection program.

Numerologists believe that the exact name you were given at birth, even if there is an error in spelling, is the name vibration you carry with you through your whole life. So, regardless of the personal or professional reasons surrounding your name change, only your given name should be used to calculate name-related core numbers in numerology because, to be honest, your new name is not the name you were given at birth, and it, therefore, has no power over your destiny.

Calculate Your Destiny Number

Calculating your destiny number only requires one piece of vital information; your exact and full name, as it was written on your birth certificate, or if you happen to fall into any of the special categories mentioned above, your name as it appeared on your school documents as a child. Here is a step-by-step way to calculate your destiny number:

1. Write down the letters in your name, making sure to leave ample space between your first, middle name(s), and last name/family name. This is important so that you are able to add up the number in small chunks.

2. Underneath each letter for every name, pen down the number vibrations that coincide with the letters written down. Refer to the Pythagorean chart in chapter 9 for further clarification. Remember that suffixes and generational references are not to be included, and extra letters similar to but not part of the English alphabet should be calculated as the letters closest to it in the chart. So, ö should be read as O, ä as A, and Æ as A and E, respectively.

3. Sum up the number vibrations in your first name and reduce the number down to a single digit. Do the same for your middle and last names.

4. To get your destiny number, add up the numerical values of the reduced digits from your first, middle, and last names and reduce the resulting figure to a single digit.

For instance, let's calculate the destiny number of an imaginary person called Mary-Anne Clark.

Mary: 4 + 1 + 9 + 7 = 21; 2 + 1 = 3

Anne: 1 + 5 + 5 + 5 = 16; 1 + 6 = 7

Clark: 3 + 3 + 1 + 9 + 2 = 18; 1 + 8 = 9

What is the destiny number of the 44th president of the United States, Barack Hussein Obama?

Barack: 2 + 1 + 9 + 1 + 3 + 2 = 18; 1 + 8 = 9

Hussein: 8 + 3 + 1 + 1 + 5 + 9 + 5 = 32; 3 + 2 = 5

Obama: 6 + 2 + 1 + 4 + 1 = 14; 1 + 4 = 5

Barack Obama has a destiny number of 1. From his chart, you can see the number 1 appears multiple times, indicating leadership, innovation, and a pioneering attitude. The number 5 also appears multiple times, showing that he is the type of person who loves to be active, creative, and busy. Do the numbers not fit his personality profile?

Destiny numbers are fun things to calculate. Bear in mind that they don't just affect humans. Destiny numbers can tell or affect the personality profile of pets too. That sassy cat of yours who wants its dinner at a particular time and will go to any length to get your attention, such as blocking your view while you watch a rerun of your favorite show or meowing while staring at the clock, may be number one.

The Meanings of Different Destiny Numbers

(1)

Determined, independent, and self-sufficient, you rule the roost. You have a competitive spirit and will do whatever it takes to succeed. Your authenticity and "take-no-prisoners" approach toward fulfilling your potential make people see you as the dictatorial sort. They are not wrong because you tend to like your own ideas better than anyone else's.

You enjoy the outdoors and freedom and dislike it when people put restrictions on you or keep tabs on you. You are unafraid of standing out from the crowd, whether it's through fashion, speech, or your unique approach to doing things. You love being the center of attention, and for you, compliments always go a long way towards buttering you up.

It is imperative for you to remember that the opinions of others matter. You might even learn a thing or two from others. Curb your tyrannical tendencies. Life isn't a ship where you have to bark out commands to get things done. Gentle persuasion may be far from your usual approach, but it wouldn't hurt to try it once in a while.

(2)

Insightful, cultured, intuitive, refined, and sensitive, you are the kind that has tact down pat. You could sashay into any space and effectively read the room. This is not just handy for organizing seating arrangements at weddings. Your intuition and sensitivity allow you to constructively use your words so as not to hurt someone else. You are a wonderful listener. Everyone finds themselves spilling their guts at your feet while you heal them using your words and empathy.

You enjoy being the steady force backstage, influencing others to be the best version of themselves, as opposed to the number one who wants to be at the front and center of every parade. You can be trusted to juggle multiple tasks at once and still be on time for that appointment without breaking a sweat. You thrive when working in partnership with others.

You are not troublesome by nature, but you can't stand it when people take advantage of you or others, and you have no qualms about shutting perpetrators out. You are a student of life. People can depend on you to know the weirdest facts as you are constantly collecting and curating knowledge.

During your service to others, remember to set firm boundaries for your own personal and mental health needs. Don't say yes when you mean no. Also, control your tendency to sulk when offended. After all, people make mistakes, and a lot of people will step on your tender feet (and heart).

(3)

Optimism, enthusiasm, friendship, self-expression, and happiness are the backbone of anyone with a destiny number of 3. You love life and are not afraid to show it. Your zest for life, just like your aura and laughter, is contagious. You can raise the energy of any room you walk into, and as a result, the party does not start until you have walked in.

You have the gift of the robe and are aware that persuasion is more effective than force in getting you what you want. As a result, you improve your argument rather than raising your voice. You can sell ice to an Eskimo.

Your eternal youthfulness and child-like nature could make you petulant at times. For instance, you could play pranks but not like them as much when the favor is returned.

You enjoy attention from others and play up your appearance to get it. Because you enjoy being everyone's friend, you may find yourself juggling more responsibilities than you think you are able to handle.

Try as much as you can to keep your engagements and commitments to a minimum. Do not take on more than you are able to handle effectively. Time management, concentrating your energies, and being more responsible are in your best interests. Enthusiasm is nice, but you need to learn practicality.

(4)

If there was ever a number that could be likened to a mountain, this would be it. You are steady, reliable, structured, dependable, and practical. Patience, diligence, and perseverance are your mantras. You can be trusted to complete every task laid out for you, even if it takes you some time to finish. The elephant has nothing on you when it comes to recall. You can remember even the most insignificant things. It is both your blessing and your curse.

As a detail-oriented person, you work best when there is a timetable, list, method, or routine for you to follow. This is sometimes a bad thing because routines (and consequently you) are not very amenable to change. The slightest change in a process you are used to can throw you off your game, so you are not the most adaptable fellow on the planet.

Your honest, sincere, and down-to-earth nature makes you one of the best friends anyone can have, as they can be sure to stick by you through thick and thin. You are very conscious of your time and finances. This quality of yours makes you a super saver, but on the flip side, your frugal nature stops you from experiencing the best life has to offer. It's fun to partake in something frivolous once in a while. There! I said it. Wipe the look of horror from your face and whip out that bucket list you have tossed to the bottom of the drawer.

(5)

Like the pentagram that points in five directions at the same time, you are the king or queen of multitasking. You can talk on the phone, watch TV, cook dinner, and read a book all at the same time. This quality of yours is possibly due to your dislike of routine (how odd that it follows the number 4) and monotony. You are always full of restless and pent-up energy. Even in bed, your mind is never asleep.

In contrast to the rigid lists needed by 4, you require change and variety to function well. You are not only multitalented – but also multifaceted. Your inquisitive nature causes you to question everything. The irony, however, is the fact that you dislike people questioning you. You are impulsive, creative, spontaneous, and will leave a venue or a person that is dull to you before anyone can say, Jack. You may be a walking, breathing party waiting to happen at a moment's notice, but my advice to you is to slow down, take the time to smell the roses, and think of all the wonderful experiences you have missed because you are always in a hurry. Sometimes a night at home does more good than a party at the club.

(6)

Affectionate, nurturing, and loving, a 6 will always leave you better than they found you. Your mantra is, "Let peace reign on earth, and may it start with me." You are responsible, reliable, and enjoy catering to others. Your hospitality and integrity know no bounds, even when it comes to people you've just met and barely know.

You have an amiable and even-tempered personality, you do not shy away from volunteering, and you're always happy to take on more than your share of the responsibility. You are attracted to music, art, and nature. You also have a keen eye for color and design. You love the good life and are not afraid to shell out the big bucks for your comfort.

While caring for others is ideal, practice self-love because you also need attention and care. Don't be in a hurry to give out unsolicited advice. Sometimes people just want to work things out for themselves. Your need for materialistic comforts should not overshadow your logic. I am sure you can wait for a sale on that cashmere sweater or strike a bargain for your favorite bottle of bubbly.

(7)

A typical 7 reminds me of Spencer Reid from the show Criminal Minds. Remember the smart dude who saw patterns in everything and always had his nose buried in a file, book, or board? You're intelligent, analytical, and able to retain large amounts of information. Your skeptical nature ensures that you never believe anything at face value or via hearsay, which is just as well because you dislike gossip and gossipmongers. You will always require proof. You won't even believe someone died until you see the body.

You are a loner who uses solitude to recharge your batteries. You always appear cold and aloof, but you feel things deeply and are one of the best and most loyal friends one could have. I have met 7s who appear frigid but are loving and caring dog or cat dads. Your aristocratic bearing and refined tastes complement your desire for perfection in all you do. You are an old soul attracted to the unknown and the spiritual.

You believe in the law of karma and, because of this, strive to walk on the straight and narrow even when no one is watching. It might be painful to hear this as a 7, but you need to widen your social circle. This will only happen when you learn the art of small talk and understand that it's alright to approach people for conversation first. Stay away from antidepressants, intoxicants, and stimulants. Your mental constitution is usually more affected than others by these substances since you are almost always melancholy.

(8)

8 is an ambitious, money-driven business tycoon who has a lot of goals and little or no patience for dreams. You are a skilled manager and organizer who works well under pressure and keeps a level head in times of emergency. You are capable of handling any task,

but you become irate when you are micromanaged. Instead, you love to be the one marshaling out orders instead.

You are quite conscious of your diet, physical health, and fitness, and you monitor them daily. That, and the fact that a polished appearance screams wealth and status. As an 8, if the letters Z, H, or Q do not appear in your given name, you have a tendency to rapidly gain or lose weight under stress.

Tact is necessary even at work. When you give others a chance to express their opinions, you are more likely to command the respect due to you. Also, find time to balance your life. As a workaholic, your nose is always on the grindstone, and as such, you have little or no time for extracurricular activities or romance. Go out there and have fun; the world can wait!

(9)

A visionary and a humanitarian, you have a deep appreciation for art, music, culture, beauty, and nature. You have the ability to influence and tolerate others, which is why you don't understand why everyone else can't get along. You are either widely traveled or a geography buff with knowledge of diverse people, cultures, and food. You are caring, generous, and kind-hearted, always willing to help others or give freely of yourself to whoever asks.

You are extremely loyal in partnerships – but forming one-on-one relationships can be a bit of a hassle. The wisdom you are blessed with is a result of having weathered a lot of difficulties and bad experiences in life. Learn to forgive others who offend you or who are not as thoughtful or as generous as you are. People are wired differently, and as a number 9, the most precious gift you can give to the world is total acceptance and selfless service.

(11)

11 is a master number, which means it has a higher and stronger vibration than destiny number 2. Spiritual, idealistic, and highly imaginative, you have immense capability to influence people and

events. The energy of 1 means you enjoy being in the spotlight, leading, and managing people.

You are highly intelligent and a great listener with superior powers of communication. As a highly imaginative and curious person, you are here to learn everything the world has to teach you. You spend more time daydreaming than achieving any set goals. Your enhanced levels of intuition and extrasensory perception enable you to align yourself with a higher purpose, one that makes a difference in this world.

Your ability to weave stories predisposes you to the habit of compulsive lying, embellishment, and exaggeration. Also, you tend to be self-righteous and critical of others, forgetting that your path is to shine a light, not to point fingers.

(22)

The dedicated, inspirational, focused, and charismatic master number 22 is a forward-thinking visionary who, in their quest for mastery, constantly converts dreams into solid reality to reach a higher level of consciousness. 22s are practical loners that combine the creativity and intuition of 1 with the compassion and sensitivity of 2 with the tenacity and determination of 4 to make dreams a reality.

As long as you do not let your crippling fear of failure sneak up on you, the world is your oyster. Your workaholic tendencies will burn you out before you have a chance to achieve whatever it is that you desire. Like number 4, you are extremely self-righteous and high-strung. Be more accommodating of others as you put your many talents to good use.

(33)

This master number is a higher vibration or octave of the number 6. The evolved 33s are on this plane to raise the awareness and consciousness of everyone through their experiences and acts of selfless service.

The perfectionist nature of the 6 combined with the double dose of carefree attitude and sensitivity from the 3 results in the 33 being a high achiever who, unfortunately, seeks the validation of others. A fully evolved 33 is one who has completely embraced their imperfections and detaches from their personal feelings to create a positive change in the world. It is safe to say that evolved 33s are very rare as it is quite easy to fall prey to negative means of self-expression such as gossiping, complaining, and criticizing.

Chapter 11: The Soul Urge Number

The soul number (also called the soul urge, soul desire, or heart's desire number) is one of your numerology chart's most important core numbers. The soul number is the reduced sum of the digits represented by the vowels in your birth name. Unlike your destiny or personality number, the soul urge number is a mirror to your soul and a direct reflection of your given name. Embracing and tapping into this energy is important because it is an echo of the deepest desires of your subconscious mind. This number discloses your innermost desires, thoughts, habits, and baseline responses to stimuli. Only the soul number reflects the core of your soul, what you care about or crave the most in this world to feel content. It is a number indicative of your hopes, wishes, and dreams – and represents your personality in relationships.

How to Calculate the Soul Urge Number

Calculating your soul urge number requires that you extract the vowels present in your given name. The values of the vowels as they appear in the Pythagorean chart are:

- A = 1
- E = 5
- I = 9
- O = 6
- U = 3
- Y = 7

A harmony between your life path number and your soul urge number helps you to easily make decisions. Any discordance between the two means that you will be conflicted in many of the choices you have to make because of the ongoing war between your head and your heart. On the rare occasions where both numbers are the same, living your most authentic life becomes a piece of cake.

The rat race called life can dull the calling of your soul, making it difficult to understand what it is your soul truly longs for. This is why certain practices such as yoga, qigong, conscious meditation, and quiet alone time are essential. These activities not only feed the soul, but they also allow it to make its needs known to you via your intuition. All you have to do is open your heart and really listen.

The soul urge number is calculated using the vowels in your name as it appears on the birth certificate. When calculating soul numbers in numerology, consider the system used in the calculation. For instance, in Chaldean numerology, Y is considered a vowel, while in the western system, it is a consonant sometimes and a vowel at other times. In Western numerology, Y is considered a vowel when there is a lack of vowels in that particular syllable or if the letter Y is sandwiched between or next to two consonants, as seen in names like Yvette, Wynn, or Lacy. In names like these, the Y sound is pronounced as "ee." Other numerologists consider Y a vowel when it comes before another vowel in a name or syllable so that both Y and the said vowel together provide the vowel sound. This is seen in names like Doyle, Tracey, Emily, etc.

To confuse you even further, certain practitioners consider the letter W to be a vowel when it is followed by another vowel in a name or syllable so that together they provide the vowel sound, or in a case where W appears sandwiched in between two vowels. These conflicting theories make for a dizzy head, so my advice is that you go with whatever feels right to you.

Reducing-Down Method

- **Step 1:** Extract the vowels from your birth certificate's name and attach the numerical values for each of the vowels.

- **Step 2:** Sum up the numerical values from the extracted vowels, adding the vowels in each name separately, so they form individual totals.

- **Step 3:** Add up the double-digit totals for each name (unless they add up to a master number) and reduce them to a single digit. You could also decide, in this method, to add the double-digit compound number (total) and then reduce it to a single digit.

Example: A B R A H A M L I N C O L N

1 1 1 9 6

(1+1+1=3) (9+6=15; 1+5=6)

3 + 6= 9

Abraham Lincoln's soul urge number is 9.

Also, remember that it is totally your choice to reduce master numbers 11, 22, or 33 down to 2, 4, and 6, respectively. Some practitioners leave master numbers as is wherever they appear in a numerology chart, while others reduce them further down.

The Adding-Across Method

The adding across method is the most widely used. It involves you adding up the sum total of the numerical values of the vowels in your name and adding them across. After this, you reduce it to a single digit (with the exception of master numbers). Both methods of calculation reveal the same answer.

Example: A B R A H A M L I N C O L N 1+1+1+9+6= 18 (1+8) = 9

1 1 1 9 6

Your soul number represents the aspects of you that the rest of the world rarely gets to see. It could indicate the traits and talents you possess, whether or not they are developed, exhibited, or dormant, as well as your feelings or attitude towards others, love, and relationships. Understanding your soul urge number is the key to realizing the hidden aspects of you and the different levels of your inner nature, some of which you fear others finding out about as it may cause you some level of embarrassment or ridicule.

Knowing the soul numbers of your loved ones will enhance family and personal relationships as you will relate better with them, knowing why they do what they do and what feeds the desires of their soul. For instance, that tough and buff friend of yours with a soul number of 2 may not want others to find out that he bawls his eyes out during sappy scenes in movies. In the same way, your boss with a soul number of 6 may not want it made public that he has a soft spot for children, older people, and cute animals. This is why this number is a core number in the chart. It helps you know what drives people and enables you to relate to them in ways they can understand.

When calculating your soul urge number, use all the names on your birth chart. Yes, even if you have two or more middle names separated by a hyphen. If you are calculating by hand, turn your sheet of paper horizontally (landscape instead of portrait) so it contains more letters in this situation.

Soul Urge Number 1

Strong Leadership Skills: This number implies charisma, individuality, self-sufficiency, and independence. A number 1 is confident in their abilities and unbothered by the fact that they have to make tough calls from time to time. A soul urge of 1 means your deepest desire is to lead, not follow. Your strong leadership tendencies, ability to thrive in fast-paced environments, and creative spark mean that you can wield vibrations that manifest anything you set your mind to.

For this reason, people look up to you. Some may even envy you. But while your deepest desire may be leadership, you must take note of the influence of other numbers on your chart and their interaction with your soul urge number. This is because your chart may show your heart wants one thing and your head wants another. The key is to find harmony and work in alignment with your wisdom while referring to the numbers on the chart. Do this, and success will naturally gravitate towards you.

Charisma: Whether you want it or not, everyone wants a piece of you. For this reason, you are often the center of attention regardless of how you act or attempt to be a wallflower. This is because the energy of one has two major traits; leadership and the ability to influence others. As a leader, being thoughtful and caring towards your team or tribe is as natural to you as breathing. Your compelling and authentic personality is magnetic and commands respect.

Enthusiasm: Your level of intelligence means you put in the work to research topics that people often gloss over. As a result, it is difficult to get you excited about anything. However, when you have your hopes up about something, you have a way of winning people over, infecting everyone with a healthy level of motivation and excitement. It is possible that you may have eccentric or controversial views, but you always have a way to push your unique perspective onto people, convincing anyone that a healthy dose of controversy is essential to success.

Feeling Indispensable: That is when confidence has crossed the line over to arrogance. You almost never let anyone try their hand at something you want because you feel no one can do a better job than you can. This may work for you sometimes, but the greatest leaders need loyal followers, and no one is going to be loyal for too long to someone with a domineering personality.

Soul Urge Number 2

Sensitive: Is your heart allergic to the news? Do you cry at the sad scenes in movies? Are you the first to kiss and make up after an argument? If you have done the calculations and ended up with soul urge number 2, then you are an intuitive and sensitive soul. Your innermost desire is to love and be loved in return. You may dislike your emotional nature, but it is your greatest asset. Because without emotional sensitivity, there can be no intuition. And intuition gets you out of tough situations before they even occur. Embrace your heart and trust your gut because it is always spot-on.

You are the loyal and faithful sidekick, the yin to number 1's yang. You represent everything that number one isn't, and that is not a bad thing. Whereas number 1 is individualistic and a trailblazer, number 2 is sensitive and interested in harmony and balance. You don't have to be the center of attention. The spotlight could be behind the scenes too. You feel under-appreciated, but there is no 1 without a 2. All leaders need someone steady, stable, and reliable whom they trust.

The Need for Harmony: As a born peacemaker, you have an innate need for peace and harmony in life. You're the one always resolving conflicts and smoothing out ruffled feathers. Never allow your need for balance to stop you from expressing your opinions, especially when the occasion calls for you to speak your mind or defend yourself. Regardless of what others think, people will listen to you and like you even when they disagree with your point of view.

Strong Level of Intuition: many times, you wish you could feel less than you do. Never regard your strong intuition as a burden, but rather as a means of guiding those you care about. Let go of your self-doubt, connect with your intuition, and trust the process. Many people will flock to you for your wise counsel.

Soul Urge Number 3

Charisma: The French phrase "joie de vivre" is personified as soul urge number 3. These charismatic, witty individuals come with an inbuilt desire to entertain others and express themselves. They are popular in all the circles they find themselves in, and they leave an unforgettable impression on others. Like the butterfly, you are always perching from flower to flower, receiving compliments, and basking in as much attention as you can. As much as you love the trappings of luxury, you are quite adaptable to the constant surprises life brings. You live not in the moment but in *the second*, never worrying about what tomorrow may bring. Your deepest desire is to develop and express your brand of magic.

Born Entertainers: Put a soul urge 3 in a small gathering and give it a few minutes - they will convert that gathering into a sizable crowd. Their magnetism is infectious. Their happy, chatty, slightly eccentric, and outgoing nature ensures that people keep coming back for more. However, your tendency to chat may also lead you to overshare when you are anxious or tell lies for no reason whatsoever. Resist the temptation to always be the performer in every social situation you find yourself in. Slowing down does not mean you have lost your touch.

Innate Creativity: soul urge 3s can't help the creative streak they are born with. For them, self-expression and artistic flair come naturally. This is why they are easily bored by menial or routine jobs; their nature strongly forbids it, gravitating instead towards careers that allow them to utilize whatever unique talents they have. They may love money, but it is certainly not their motivation in choosing a career. Their charm and wit help them make all the right connections for success.

Soul Urge Number 4

Hard Work and Discipline: The main traits of soul urge 4 are stability, reliability, punctuality, and productivity. The typical foursome is a stickler for routines that scream practicality. To them, hard work is the backbone of success, and they are willing to invest copious amounts of time and effort to achieve their goals.

The need for structure: You thrive well in environments or setups that have a known organizational hierarchy. People depend heavily on you because you always get the job done. You are always on time, and you have no qualms about picking up the slack for others or assuming extra responsibilities. You take care of your body, your loved ones, your living quarters, and your mind. The play-by-play keeps you anchored somewhat. The only problem with your methods is that the slightest change to your routines can leave you destabilized and unhinged.

Working toward a Goal: You are always working towards something. There is no time for recreation or leisure. Although this is awesome for achieving goals, your social life suffers. You may not be a trailblazer like 1 or as creative as 3, but you notice every last detail and fine-tune any plan to perfection. You are happy to blend into your surroundings and are not interested in the spotlight, but if anyone tries to disorganize your carefully crafted image or process, they automatically become a threat, and you won't let go without a fight.

Soul Urge Number 5

Talented and creative, Soul Urge 5 is multitalented, intelligent, and has varied interests. They are the very definition of thinking outside the box. Their unconventional thoughts help them grasp even the most complex concepts quickly, while their eccentric ways and zest for life ensure they are never short of company. Their innermost desire is to travel, explore, and learn as much as they can.

Spontaneous: Only a 5 would change course halfway to their destination and have their agents on speed dial while at it. Your restless energy craves freedom at all costs, and you take risks with everything. Life is always a roller coaster for you. Many perceive you as highly unreliable because of the way you change your mind on a whim. You have so much reserved energy and passion that it is difficult to find an outlet for it all. You change careers and relationships at the drop of a hat, possibly because the thrill of the chase is more interesting to you than the end result.

The Need for Freedom: Your need for freedom is paramount. It's not something you hide from anyone who gets close to you. You dislike being under any restrictions, and commitments don't come easily to you. You never finish what you start. You are tolerant of others. You are a riot, but life is never boring for or with you.

Soul Urge Number 6

All about Others: Soul urge number 6: immersing themselves in the needs of others, so they lose sight of what they want too. Their trusting and caring nature sometimes makes them oblivious to the world around them. In the end, they put their trust in the wrong people.

Nurturing: 6 spends a lot of time nurturing others. Relationships and love affairs with other people are usually very tedious, time-consuming, and complicated for them. Unconditional love is something that they understand. This is why they can keep their promises of fidelity and loyalty to the people they care about. Letting go does not come easily for them. Ending a relationship may feel like the foundations of the relationship have been thrown out of whack. But sometimes, it has to happen to make sure that the people in their lives are worth the time and effort.

Traditional Values: You love tradition, family values, nature, and pets. You are a peacemaker who strives for harmonious relationships and cooperation. Wealth may not be foremost in your mind, but you treasure financial and emotional stability. You are big on commitments, and your word is your bond.

Soul Urge Number 7

Organizing: 7 is the soul-urge number of the controller. You have a very strong will and a deep faith in your competence. All you need is enough confidence in yourself to overcome obstacles and achieve success. For this reason, you are usually an excellent organizer and planner. You are also not afraid to be openly critical of others. This comes with incredible persuasion abilities. You can easily convince people if you want it badly enough.

Perfection: Born leaders or people who take the lead around the world, their influence will spread far and wide if they can make it happen by their efforts alone. This is a very ambitious person with a hunger for power and control. He/she may be domineering, overbearing, and aggressive. They may make such a lasting impression on people that they leave them little opportunity to react or breathe.

Integrity: Integrity is of the utmost importance to you. You are likely to have absolute faith in your beliefs and principles. You can also be brutally honest, even if it hurts the person receiving your criticism. Yours is probably not the best personality type for teamwork because you like to take charge, and you do not want anyone second-guessing your decisions.

Soul Urge Number 8

Giving: 8 is the soul-urge number of the giver. This is a person who has a sense of belonging that they find in people. Their love for others is unconditional and open-minded. They are warm and caring, with a true sense of community and humanity. 8 gives to others without expecting anything in return. They feel better when they have given—a drive in this direction towards selfless love is something that no one can deny or resist.

You Are Very Much in Touch with Your Emotions: Idealistic and passionate, you follow your heart into love affairs even if they do not go where you expect or wish they would. You are the type of person that you would not care to have as a friend or love interest. You can be very fickle and often act on instinct rather than logic. If you feel it is right to do so, you make decisions based on what feels good at the time, not necessarily what is right.

You're Non-Materialistic: you have a very open mind and are not interested in material things like money or status. You will take on many causes throughout your lifetime, even if they prove to be difficult or thankless tasks. Your desire to give your all for others is always present and remains until the end of your days. You are a true humanitarian, and your heart is always in the right place. You have no interest in owning many things or having a lot of wealth, regardless of how much money you make. This is something that you have in common with people who have the same soul urge number and who feel as if they have enough material goods to last them for their lifetime or for multiple lifetimes. But that does not mean you are not interested in helping others out. In fact, you are more than willing to give selflessly to those around you once you get the chance.

You Live Life by Your Own Rules and Beliefs: Yours is a personality full of energy, determination, purpose, and initiative. You have the drive and determination to achieve whatever you set your mind to.

Soul Urge Number 9

A visionary and dreamer, 9 is the soul-urge number of the visionary. They are dreamers of big dreams and have a natural ability to see into the hearts of people and situations. 9 has an instinct that tells them when things may be changing for the better or worse in their lives. Their intuition about people can be seen through their unerring sense of knowing who they can trust and who they cannot. They are willing to take risks in life by giving themselves over to others and going to places where they may not otherwise go. Traveling and learning new things are also part of their soul urge.

Busy Body: 9s are hyperactive souls who seem to never be at rest, even when they are sleeping. They always have something going on in their minds and in their lives. You may find them running from one project to the next without being able to sit still long enough to really take a deep breath.

Social Butterfly: The majority of 9s love being around other people and thrive on interaction with others without having a need for solitude or quiet time on the side. They have a capacity for leadership but can also be very comfortable following another's instructions if necessary.

The overall lesson of number nine is based on giving (9 + 1 = 10, 1 + 0 = 1), learning to say no, doing things that scare you, overcoming self-imposed limitations, and letting go of the past. For some people, the journey to learning these life lessons will be long and hard, but those who do will gain tremendous wisdom from the experience that can be applied for the rest of their lives.

The Universal Law of Karma: You're here to learn fulfillment. This universal law is based on the more basic principle of cause and effect. Whatever we think, say, or do has causes that affect our lives in some way. These can be seen as good effects or bad effects depending on how we see ourselves, the world, and all of life around us.

Chapter 12: Your Personality Number

In Numerology, the personality number is among the five fundamental numbers.

It's probably safe to say that the personality number is the least known of the two primary numbers sourced from the destiny, or expression number (also known as the "Total Name number"). The other is the Soul Urge Number – and, whereas the Soul Urge Number is calculated solely on the basis of the vowels in your full name in childhood, the Personality Number is determined solely on the basis of consonants.

The Personality Number: What Does It Mean?

That this is the most important number is fairly self-explanatory—it describes the persona. When interacting with other people around the world, your distinguishing characteristics and qualities help to define who you are. As a result, it frequently and uncannily describes the individual's individual style and favorite attire.

It's interesting to note that some modern numerologists refer to this number as the "Quiet Self." They do not use it as a predictor of outward behavior but rather as a marker of what an individual hopes to accomplish in the outside world.

When it comes to an understanding of oneself and also being able to master affirmation, self-compassion, and self-love, the number zero must be taken into account.

In addition, learning more about this tiny section of your numerology chart can provide you with helpful hints on how to improve, grow, and mature in certain areas of your life.

Calculating Your Personality Number

There are two ways to do this. First, you can subtract your soul urge number from your destiny number using Pythagorean numerology. When you use this method, you're not going to get numbers 11 or 22 unless you make use of the subtotals.

The other method is to add all the numerological values of your name's consonants and continue to sum them up till you reduce them to a master number or a single digit. Keep in mind that you can't get this number using your married name or your nickname. You have to use the full name on your birth certificate, including your middle name. Even if your name is misspelled, you must use it as it is. For your convenience, here are the consonants and their values:

- A – 1
- B – 2
- C – 3
- F – 6
- G – 7
- H – 8
- J – 1
-
- K – 2
- L – 3
- M – 4
- N – 5
- P – 7
- Q – 8
- R – 9
- S – 1
- T – 2
- V – 4
- W – 5
- X – 6
- Z – 8

As for the letter Y, sometimes it's a consonant, sometimes it's a vowel. It all depends on the word it is in and how it sounds. For instance, Y is a consonant when it takes the place of a hard consonant sound, like Yolanda, Toyota, and so on. Y can also follow a vowel, in which case it's not a consonant, as is the case in words like Maya, Gray, and Kaysha.

Personality Numbers and Meanings

Personality Number 1 is a person who stands out from the crowd.

This numerology number is a good choice for a leader. They are honorable and lovable because they are number one. In general, they possess outstanding characteristics.

A number 1 is a fearless leader who possesses exceptional levels of resilience and stamina. They are extremely effective and are always at the vanguard of all they do. They have been endowed with the capacity to manage people and see endeavors through to completion.

Personality Number 2 is a gregarious and outgoing individual.

The central message of this number is that of friendship and companionship. Number 2s are aesthetically pleasing, gentle, and meticulous in their attention to detail. It is the function of number 2 to act as a mediator. They are dependable and reasonable. Since they are calm, gentle, and credible, people in the number 2 position make excellent mediators. Also noteworthy is the fact that this numerology is remarkably down-to-earth, pleasant, and attentive. Their sensitive personalities allow them to be extremely patient.

Personality number 3 is a character with a distinct personality.

This number has a remarkable ability to communicate thoughts and feelings. They are friendly and chatty – and amazingly talented in the arts. People who fall into the third category are eternal optimists, which makes them a delightful and enjoyable presence. With this numerology, it is simple to express love and affection. They are excellent conversationalists who exude enthusiasm and enthusiasm for their work. Additionally, they are excellent listeners.

Personality Number 4 is a character with a unique personality.

The number 4 represents someone who is hardworking, serious, and practical. These individuals have a high level of dependability, reliability, and credibility. They have a strong attachment to their families and to their community. Many people believe that the number 4 represents a highly dedicated person. People with this numerology possess a strong desire to learn – and are respectful and dedicated to the core. The number 4 personality is characterized by its inner strength and determination.

Personality number 5 is the freedom-loving, adaptable, and adventurous type.

The number 5s are a unique breed. Originality, quick-fire wit, and a dash of nervous energy characterize this individual's presence, making them unforgettable. Interactions with this number are exhilarating and elicit deep thought from the participants. When they share their ideas, they are bursting with enthusiasm, and their limitless energy serves as an inspiration to those around them.

Personality number 6 has sympathy and compassion as the overarching themes that run through it.

The roles of defender and caregiver bring great satisfaction to this individual. When it comes to number 6, you can lean heavily on them for help because of their loving disposition; they have a high level of responsibility, are generous, and make excellent counselors. The number 6 exudes calmness and patience and can bring people together in a group setting. People turn to them for comfort when things are going wrong.

Personality number 7 has the appearance of being an outsider or a loner.

They are sociable once you get to know them, despite their outward appearance. This person is extremely perceptive, and they are interested in how things work. They are people who are interested in learning new things. People who fall into the seventh category are driven by a desire to learn and to ask difficult questions. Because they are highly philosophical, they may come across as incomprehensible. People pay attention to them because of their inherent wisdom, despite appearing to be secretive and sometimes difficult to understand. The words of people who are assigned the number 7 are frequently profound.

Personality number 8 is an interesting one. When it comes to taking on executive positions of influence, this number makes a strong impression on others.

They have a global perspective, are friendly, and are optimistic. Number 8s have a strong sense of authority and influence. They have a commanding presence as well as an infectious enthusiasm that makes them stand out. Number 8 is a capable and hardworking individual who will gladly complete any task assigned to him. They are capable of taking on and managing large-scale projects with outstanding success.

Personality number 9 will frequently appear to be younger than their actual age.

You get the impression that they are friendly and generous. The number 9 represents dependability, selflessness, understanding, compassion, and a desire to be of service. Others can rely on this individual because they exude spiritual energy. People come to them for guidance and wisdom. They are extremely tolerant of others and have compassionate hearts.

Personality number 11 is a person with unique traits.

The master number 11 is always interested in spiritual developments. This number is extremely dedicated to spiritual matters, possessing superior intuition when compared to the average person. These individuals possess tremendous healing potential. It is possible that they will become engaged in the health and wellness industry if they aren't already.

Because of their gentle and patient nature, they make excellent friends or romantic partners. 11s exude warmth and kindness everywhere they go, enticing others to approach and become closer to them. The spirituality of the number 11 is also an important aspect of their overall personality.

Personality number 22 is a master who gets their hands dirty. Number 22 possesses both a strong intuitive side as well as a centered, practical side to them. Fashions that are both practical and long-lasting are favorites of this group. These individuals are excellent communicators who also have a strong understanding of delegation. They are usually accompanied by a large group of people who are all eager to lend a hand with whatever major project they are working on.

22s want to profoundly impact the world in which they live. They are brought into the world with untapped potential and inexhaustible inner strength. They are constantly trying to figure out what they can do to make a positive difference in other people's lives, whether it is through a business venture, a governmental policy, or a new philosophical approach.

Their primary objective in life is to contribute to the improvement of the world. In the meantime, they will continue to experiment until they discover their true calling, which will enable them to bring about the positive change they wish to see in the world.

Personality Number 33 indicates that the person who possesses that number is extremely friendly.

Such people care about other people and animals, and this is immediately evident to everyone. It may be explained by a strong sense of empathy and compassion for other people and animals. They are always willing to stand up for the underdogs and, on occasion, even play the part of martyr. People born under the number 33 have the ability to be positive role models for others because they want to bring harmony to all people and are motivated by this goal. Number 33s are known for their strong nurturing abilities. They develop into excellent counselors who are deeply committed to those near and dear to them. They take love very seriously, and they prefer long-term marriage and a warm, stable home life. Because of their compassionate nature, they are also capable of curing the wounds of others. For such people, every situation is an opportunity to learn something new, which is why they can appear to be excellent teachers at times. When they enter into an honest and warm union, they become content and are able to offer their nurturing abilities.

Chapter 13: Your Attitude Number

Your attitude number is the most important piece of your numerology chart. It is an expression of where you come from, your basic characteristics and traits, and the general outlook you have on life. It reveals what makes you who you are and gives an insight into why we do what we do.

It can also help facilitate goal setting for both personal development and general progress in life, as well as determining whether or not it's time for a change in your life. This number indicates what makes you a unique individual and how you see the world around you. It reveals how much of your personality is due to your background or situation in life and what aspects of yourself are created from your current circumstances.

How to Determine Your Attitude Number

To calculate your attitude number, all you have to do is add the numbers in your birth month and day together. You won't need your birth year for this one. As usual, you'll have to reduce the numbers down to a single digit. For instance, say you were born on December 25. Your attitude number would be:

December has 12 days.

1 plus 2 equals 3

Day: 25

2 + 5 equals 7.

7 + 3 = 10.

Reduce 10 to a single digit, and you have 1. Therefore, your attitude number is 1. In the words of one of the deepest philosophers of our time, that's "quick math."

Attitude Number 1: You're Driven

They're outgoing, social people who are all about action. They get things done and are willing to take the lead whenever necessary. They have high expectations and can be demanding at times. They're usually self-reliant, confident, ambitious, and self-assured, as well as strong-willed people who know when to follow their gut instinct instead of letting someone else lead the way. Deeply spiritual, creative, and intuitive with a strong sense of direction in life, they rarely make plans and prefer to go with the flow. They procrastinate as little as possible before going with their gut instincts rather than making plans ahead of time.

If this is your attitude number, you're the sort of person who doesn't like to seek help from others. When people think of you, terms like "driven" and "aggressive" come to mind. Sometimes people may think that you're a bit standoffish. However, this is only because you're very used to handling your own business, and you tend to be influential and a leader naturally.

Your Challenges: you're likely to be depressed, unable, or cynical if you refuse to act from a place of authenticity. If you are not currently an independent person in any aspect of your life, you must channel all of your energy towards setting yourself free, or else you will find your creativity and zest for life stifled.

Attitude Number 2: You're Persevering

People with this attitude tend to be obliging, benevolent, and pretty touchy-feely. If this is you, you're a very nice person. You're very in touch with your instincts, and you love everything mystical and otherworldly. More than anyone else, you are very aware of the vibrations and feelings that everyone around you exudes. More often than not, this means that you are influenced by the ideas and feelings of those that are physically closest to you.

Since you are very instinctual and mystical, you appear as quite an interesting individual. You have a very deep sense of empathy for people, and you are truly interested in how their lives are going. Usually, this is because you think your own life is boring, even though other people would beg to differ.

Your Challenges: You tend to take things a little too personally, and sometimes your emotions get the best of you because you are very sensitive. Try to understand that not everybody has the depth of emotional understanding that you do and that sometimes people aren't necessarily trying to hurt you but are simply ignorant.

Attitude Number 3: You're Dynamic

You're dynamic, alluring, clever, social, and savvy if you have this attitude number. You also have a wonderful sense of humor and an appreciation for the comical. More often than not, you're the life of the party. As long as you're part of a gathering, everyone's energy is positive and excited. The downside of this superpower is that everyone else feels the same way when you're in a bad mood. You never wallow in negative emotions. You're very quick to bounce back, and you often have a great time performing for people around you. This performance is not about being inauthentic but is rooted in a genuine desire to see people happy.

Your Challenges: Because you have a deep-seated fear of criticism, you might find yourself constantly keeping your dreams on the back burner. You may also do this because you have emotional baggage that weighs you down. Try to understand that no matter what you do, there will always be people who do not approve, and that is completely fine and is not a statement as to your worth. Also, it's fine to feel terrible and still take action on the things that matter to you. Usually, action will bring you out of that deep, dark well and spur you on to greatness.

Attitude Number 4: You're Sensitive

Those who have this attitude are dependable, reliable, dedicated, always faithful, and legit in all they do. You are a very grounded person, and so you're not a big fan of taking risks or surprises. For this reason, people think of you as being a little too inflexible and often assume that you don't enjoy life as much as you should. The reality of the situation is that you're simply concerned about other people and how they are doing. You are especially concerned about the people that are near and dear to your heart, and you don't want them to get wrecked by a reckless decision.

Your Challenges: Sometimes, you allow your inflexible nature to get in the way of your success. As much as stability and financial security matter to you, you can sometimes cut yourself off from avenues to success when you refuse to step outside your lane. You dare to do the unfamiliar sometimes. That is when the magic happens.

Attitude Number 5: You're Creative

When people meet you, they see someone who is brave, lively, and always bright. You have an uncanny understanding of change, and you're willing to accept it. You are very fun to be around and can be quite the coquette. You're the sort of person who enjoys being the center of attention, even if you don't necessarily struggle for it.

A brave soul is in touch with their sensitive side. You are the sort of person who's always on the lookout for new things. If something seems to be out of the ordinary, you are very drawn to it because you want to know a lot more. For this reason, you love to travel because you believe that there is a lot to experience in the world and you want to enjoy everything you can. You're probably the sort of person who says, "Try everything once."

Your Challenges: Your propensity to swing from one extreme to another can be rather disruptive if you're not careful. You tend to create unfavorable circumstances in life because you're trying to define what personal freedom means to you. The irony is that you will often create restrictions in your own life in your quest for personal freedom. To fix this problem, simply understand that you were always free. Keep your cheerful disposition and remain adventurous, even when you feel fearful. In fact, you should allow the fear to inspire you to take action anyway, and when things don't go your way, don't try to keep such a tight leash on everyone and everything.

Attitude Number 6: The Analyst

If this is you, you place friends, family, and lovers above everything else in life. You also have a deeply profound appreciation for your colleagues at work, especially when they help to make things easier for you. You have lovely healing energy around you that you can tap into if you want to. As a deeply analytical person, you tend to want to take control of all that you can, and you do this because you are particular about having perfect results. Something about you just draws many people to you.

Your Challenge: You have to learn to find balance when it comes to your sense of responsibility, especially when it comes to yourself versus other people. Because you have a tendency to be a perfectionist in all that you do, you may find that this perfectionist trait has a tendency to reduce your happiness and willingness to accept yourself or other people. Understand that you don't always have to get it right. Being flawed and making mistakes is part of the human experience.

Attitude Number 7: You're Harmonious

When people are around you, they get the sense that if they ever met Albert Einstein, he would probably be just like you. You come off as really thoughtful and scholarly, even scientific. You are very clever, and it's very obvious. You are a mystery in the flesh. The fact that you're a bit of an introvert just amplifies the mysterious aspects of you. You are usually one of the first people to notice when things are different, and you have the uncanny ability to analyze details that most people never think of.

Your Challenge: you have a tongue so sharp it can slice a molecule into a billion pieces. You can also be pretty sarcastic, often as a guide for your anger, expressing it in ways that you often playoff as a joke. However, you know, you're not kidding. You also have a tendency to be superficial about life. Try to temper your words with kindness and see things from other people's perspectives. When you feel upset, make a point of communicating that clearly and respectfully to the offending party. Also, stop being afraid of having things that matter to you in life. You can still dive deep into life experiences while maintaining an air of playfulness.

Attitude Number 8: You're Secretive

You are the one who can give the person with attitude number 1 a run for their money when it comes to leadership. There is iron in your veins, and you were very dedicated and passionate about finishing what others had begun and quit. You don't understand the meaning of the word "quit." This is why people often turn to you to lead them in major projects and situations in life, especially when it comes to politics, business, and entrepreneurial affairs. You are the ultimate provider, and you are excellent with finances. When it comes to making sure the people you love are cared for, you leave no stone unturned. If it's something that's going to make you money to be able to take care of your family, you can bet that you're interested in it because it's a little too hard for you to hold on to money for a long time. You know you have this tendency, and so you mitigate that risk by being proactive with your finances. When it comes to the way you relate to people, no one ever has to second guess what you say or wonder if you meant what you meant. This is because you're particular about being clear in your communications and leaving no room for doubt or questioning.

Your Challenge: you're not very good with authority. You're also not quite adept at letting go of hurtful and difficult things from the past. This is usually because you've had to deal with some horrific and challenging experiences from childhood, and so you continue to allow those past experiences to color your present and future. It's okay not to be the one in charge every now and then. In fact, by allowing others to shine every now and then, you show your generous and magnanimous side, and people appreciate that and will gladly let you lead, too. Also, realize that past results do not predict future outcomes and that at any moment right now, you can take charge of your life and choose something different and better.

Attitude Number 9: Prudence Personified

You are an extraordinarily gentle person who is very aware of other people's needs. If people had to describe you, they would say that you were the ultimate saint, the quintessential martyr. You're always more concerned about how everyone else is doing than yourself, and this is not from some need to be thought of as important or appreciated just because it feels good. You're a true bleeding heart in a good way, often concerned with making the world a much better place for one and all. Because of your humanitarian ideals, charisma, and social pull, you are able to bring people together and get them moving on things that will be good for the world. This makes you a very powerful leader in a different way from attitude number 8 or 1 person.

Your Challenge: because you are so in touch with people's needs and how they can live much better lives, you sometimes find yourself going through hardship. Realize that as much as you want to save the world, you can't save those who don't want to save themselves. Also, recognize which burdens are yours and which aren't and which you'll need to enlist some help for. This salvation business is not something you can do on your own, and you're going to need all the help you can get. Another problem comes you're your tendency to often fight for other people, and you tend to easily get frustrated and exhausted as a result. Every now and then, you need someone in your corner too. Let someone else take the lead. It doesn't make you a terrible person to step back and feed your soul. Remember, you can't give what you don't have.

Chapter 14: Your Heredity Number

Your hereditary number is inherited from your parents. Usually, the father's name is the more prominent one, unless your parents decided to give you your mother's last name or join their last names to give you instead. This number gives you your backstory. It allows you to understand your roots and how they can affect you for the better or for worse. They also show you the way you interact with others socially. Think of this number as the entirety of your family tree's socio-cultural heritage. It helps you understand your family's vibrational set point. To be clear, this number may not have many far-reaching implications for your own personal life, so you shouldn't beat yourself up for not having the "right family" if you're not fond of the meaning of your number. Just think of it as a number with some extra information that you can use if you want to.

How to Calculate Your Hereditary Number

This number is calculated by summing all the letters in your mother's last (maiden) name and your father's last name. Let's assume your mother's last name is Jetson and your father's last name is Hall. We're going to work with our usual letter-number correspondence.

J + E + T + S + O + N

= 1 + 5 + 2 + 1 + 6 + 5

= 20

=2

H + A + L + L

= 8 + 1 + 3 + 3

= 15

=6

2 + 6 = 8

Your hereditary number would be 8. Now, let's check out the meanings of each one.

Hereditary Number 1

This number bestows you with a lot of confidence. You can be bold about going after your dreams because you have self-assurance. This is why you are very likely to be found at the top of the food chain no matter what aspect of life you are involved in. You're probably a loner, and because of this, you need to foster a sense of independence. Your desire for independence could be touched by a bit of egotism. Despite this, the fact that you can have a lot of time to yourself means you have endless opportunities to express the boundless creativity within you. Freedom and independence allow you the room you need for self-improvement.

When it comes to working, you're a natural-born leader, and everyone thinks of you as qualified and capable. This is why whenever you decide to give guidance or instructions to others, they quickly accept them. In other words, you are a master organizer.

You're also likely to be great in business, making huge strides where others fail. You have courage that lasts centuries and an iron that will never bend, no matter what obstacles challenge it. The energy of number one means you're likely to have major success in your professional life because you have deep ambition and are desirous of climbing the social ladder. You can also be pretty prideful and sometimes even a little too domineering. Every now and then, your nerves overwhelm you.

Hereditary Number 2

Your social skills are very impressive. There's nothing you love more than being in contact with other humans. You have excellent manners in your family and outside, which means that you are a great mediator and diplomat. You understand the importance of balance and moderation in all that you do. You're also very loved by your dear ones. You're the kind of person who many people flock to, seeking your company. And it's not just because you're a very kind person. You make an excellent colleague and partner. You are trustworthy, and you have common sense in spades.

You exude kindness and harmony. You know how to take your natural, peaceful nature and use it for the greater good, and there is nothing more that you appreciate than when two people can work harmoniously together or when two enemies become friends again. You value tradition and all things that are durable and solid. Your lifestyle is luxurious and sociable for the most part. However, that does not stop you from being patient and persevering when you have to achieve your goals. You're all about the finer things in life and feeling comfortable. For this reason, you will stop at nothing to make sure that you achieve your desires. Because of how kind you are, you have to be very careful about allowing others to mistake your kindness for weakness.

Hereditary Number 3

If this is your hereditary number, you have an uncanny ability to adapt, regardless of the situation you're facing. You're also incredible at assimilation. Because of these two traits, you never have issues with being misunderstood right out of the gate. Being absolutely clear is a talent for you. While not everyone in your family may be the world's greatest orator, chances are it's easy for you to talk because you have the gift of gab. This number is all about expressing yourself skillfully, and no one can argue that you are exceptionally sociable. In fact, some might even say that you're a bit of a chatterbox.

Number three is also all about creativity. So, when it comes to your job, you have a lot of options about what you'd like to dedicate your time to. You could be an artist, actor, lawyer, teacher, publicist, storekeeper, or politician. The world is basically your oyster. Beyond your ability to communicate clearly and effectively, you also know how to integrate everything that you want to learn or have knowledge of. You're not afraid of long studies because you are naturally curious and constantly inventive.

Hereditary Number 4

If this is your number, you have an awesome future ahead of you thanks to the skills that you've got, which are great in a working environment. Part of the reason you will be successful is that you have intrinsic motivations. The only downside to having this number as your hereditary number is that there is a chance you might be tempted towards extreme situations and positions. Because this number has serious energy to it, if this is your number, you are most likely to be a very sober individual with a reasonable outlook on life. Some people may mistake you for being dull (they may have done so, especially in childhood), but that's not the case at all. When you finally decide to master this trait you have, you will be respected by all.

You may not always be in a position of leadership, but the thing about you is that you can find solutions no matter how complex a problem is. You're able to spot things that no one else can see. This is because your mind is very organized and methodical in how it processes things. You have analytic skills that can help you work through all the information. You know what makes the world tick, and you know how to harness that information for your own benefit. You will do exceptionally well in a scientific career, especially in the social and natural sciences.

There is a lot more complexity to your character than meets the eye. You're not just about the method, but order. This is why, in situations of chaos, you seek to bring balance all the time. You're a righteous person who has a very strong moral compass, but you need to be careful about being too rigid in life because that could prevent you from experiencing greatness. You're a righteous person with a strong moral compass who is able to support society as needed. However, you need to beware of being rigid in your ways because you can be rather stubborn. On the whole, you're serious, and you have great, positive energy.

Hereditary Number 5

You're the sort of person everyone respects and accepts. Regardless of the language they speak, the country they're from, or how old they are, you tend to easily turn strangers into friends. Also, these are no ordinary friends. You inspire loyalty and everyone you meet. Your ability to seamlessly integrate with everyone does not mean that you are a master hypocrite or that you're a liar and inauthentic to yourself. You are simply truly loved and appreciated because of the positive energy that you put out. Your enthusiasm and passion for life continue to propel you forward. These are the same traits that make themselves obvious even when you crack a very simple joke or you're working on a very complex project. This is why you're a lovely person to have on your side, whether times are good or bad. You're the one who always breathes the embers of a dying flame back to life, whether it's a project or relationship.

The major themes of this number are perseverance and courage. When everyone else has thrown in the towel, you're the one who continues to fight, and you won't stop until you finally succeed. You're a dynamic person who's always going to continue pushing until you make something happen, which makes you an excellent colleague, a great worker, and a lovely friend.

Your perseverance has a very deep source. It comes from your desire to never yield to your own self. People may assume that your exuberance and continued drive mean you must have no inner demons of your own, but that's far from the case. Your drive comes from your continuous battle with the monsters under your bed.

This is why, even in the face of failure, you can find sufficient courage to carry things through. Even when you're sorely tempted to quit, you keep going. However, you do need other people by your side to make sure you're not heading straight for a ditch.

Hereditary Number 6

You are the sort of person who has learned about responsibility from a young age. In fact, it's a value that your family has, and it shapes who you are as a person. You are very particular about being ethical and moral in all that you do. You have a deep sense of justice, generosity, and honesty. You're the sort of person who people can trust because you're often dependable and can even be charitable. You have a deep, sincere love for other people, and you show your kindness very often towards them. You also have a deep sense of humanity, and this makes you very amicable because you seek nothing more than harmony between one and all.

This number bestows you with the energy of compassion and kindness, which could make you lean towards philanthropic interests. There's a huge chance that you will occupy a leadership position or eventually have a position such as this. You're a magnanimous leader, too, because you're very tolerant towards others, sometimes even more so than you are towards yourself. Because of your inherent sense of justice, you are the one who champions mighty causes, looking for truth and fairness in every situation. However, you tend to be hesitant and a little uncertain when it comes to your personal life. This is why you find it really hard to make the best decisions for yourself.

Hereditary Number 7

People with this hereditary number are often deeply interested in meditation and practice it frequently. They are naturally alert to everything that happens around them. Their inner life is really rich and intense, and this can make it very easy for them to mediate situations in real life with their intuition. They are also masters of moderation and all their affairs. These individuals have incredible skills when it comes to reflection and analysis. Their natural inclination towards meditation makes it so that there are reasonable, cautious, and discreet people.

They think that the phrase "no man is an island" is absolutely ridiculous, and they love nothing more than the life of a hermit. However, this is counterbalanced by their lust and curiosity for life, so much so that every once in a while, you may catch them coming out of their shells. These people have a very uncanny run of good luck all throughout their lives. If there's ever anyone who's always at the right place, at the right time, meeting the right people under the right circumstances, it's the one with hereditary number 7.

Hereditary Number 8

This is a number of dualities. There are times when its energy is so strong that it could be overwhelming, even though it has righteous traits. Those who have this hereditary number are very strongly determined, almost to the point of being authoritative. They command respect without uttering a single word. If you need two people who strongly oppose each other to find common ground, an 8 will make them see eye to eye. The eight are also naturals at getting people to be motivated when it comes to working, and this is why they make lovely coaches, CEOs, teachers, and heads of organizations and associations.

The strength they possess needs to be controlled, and that's why the 8s need to work on themselves to create a clear demarcation between impulsiveness and determination. The worst thing about their determination is that they can quickly become stubborn in an unproductive way.

If this is your hereditary number, you must learn to listen to others and really hear what they mean. Don't be afraid to reach out to them for advice. When you can do this, you will experience a renewal of strength with the clarity others can sometimes offer you, and being willing to ask and listen will make you an even better leader than most.

This number is also all about justice and having a strong sense of morality; the eight will make sure justice is served. They have the willpower to enforce fairness in all situations, and this is why they can't stand anything that smacks of spite or ego. They have to learn, though, that if they're not careful, they may see evil everywhere and come down so hard on it that they become the villain themselves, or at the very least, come off as obnoxious to most.

Hereditary Number 9

Those who have this number have a sense of self-respect and honor that can't be matched. When it comes to dealing with others, love, altruism, and self-esteem lead the way. They've learned how to enter or come out of all situations with their heads held high and their dignity intact. This penchant for dignity is strong in its roots. The one downside is that sometimes dignity can become pride, and it could stop them from seeing what needs to be seen or being who they need to be to advance in life.

This number has an aura of nobility about it, the sort you don't learn but naturally exude. It's rooted in empathy and devotion. The nine have a head full of generous insights that could lead them headlong into humanitarian cause after cause. As far as this number is concerned, solidarity is always the watchword, and so they're very quick to share what they have, no matter how little that may be. The furthest thing from materialistic, these people can't be swayed by offers of riches or fame or any of the shiny things the world tries to tell us are important. They are able to look at themselves and their thoughts holistically, and so they make excellent philosophers.

This number loves to travel to far-off, strange places. They love adventure, moving from pin to pin all over the map. What drives them most to move is their desire to learn about different cultures and minds, to see the differences in perspectives, and find the common threads that bind us all. They love lyricism and always welcome the opportunity to grow because, as far as they're concerned, there's no point to life if they can't be better than who they were yesterday.

Chapter 15: Numerology and Compatibility

You can use numerology to verify whether or not you and someone else are romantically compatible with each other. You don't have to just rely on sun signs, moon signs, and rising signs in astrology to find out your compatibility with someone. You can use your numbers because they're a very accurate representation of your energy and what you're about, and therefore, they can tell you how well you can blend with someone else and if your relationship has a future.

Now, to be absolutely clear, you can find love with any number, so please don't be one of those people who say, "I could never date a Scorpio" or something to that effect with numerology. All relationships require work when it comes right down to it. No one said it had to be easy, and Disney is not an accurate barometer to measure your love with. Love doesn't always have to last either, but you'll come to learn things about yourself within - and after -each relationship you're in. Love makes you grow, and it doesn't have to last forever or remain the same to do that.

Compatibility through the Lens of Numerology

When you want to work out how compatible you are with someone, using numerology, you should begin with these numbers:

- The Life Path number
- The Expression number
- The Soul Urge number

When you compare these numbers of yours with someone else's, you can quickly figure out whether or not they're a good fit—again, from the point of view of numerology. You'll know whether your ways of expressing yourselves will be a good fit or if you're likely to keep locking horns with each other.

If you're wondering if your relationship will last, there's a chance numerology can answer that question for you. However, I should mention that having to ask that question may mean you need to pause for a moment and think about what could be driving you to wonder about its longevity. Could it be that this person you're with began as a rebound that you hadn't meant to take seriously? Or are you still finding it hard to trust in love?

Another thing could be that you're both madly in love with each other, but circumstances make it, so you have no choice but to keep traveling away from each other, or you live in entirely different states. You may be wondering if things will work out for you. In this case, it's helpful to have your relationship number. You can also use numerology to learn about your partner, their needs, how you can both build a life together or amicably part ways, and so on.

Combos and Compatibility

Before we get into this, you need to know that you shouldn't be so quick to dismiss someone as being bad for you if - at first blush - it seems like you don't mesh well at all. Remember, you're talking about two people here, and the thing about people is that they're complicated. Remember, the idea is to compare each person's life path, expression, and soul urge numbers with the other's. If it seems like some numbers have been skipped, they haven't. There's no sense in looking at the 1 and 2 combinations only to look at the 2 and 1 again. With that in mind, let's get to it.

1 and 1

This is a powerful combination as long as no one feels like the other person is overpowering them. You both have very powerful ambitions, and sometimes this can cause some flooding and friction between you two. There is also a chance that you might both grow resentful of each other. However, when you give each other respect and space to be yourselves, it's possible for you to build something lovely. When it comes to clarity in communication, you're both going to find it easy to state what you want, and this means that your partnership is going to be full of honesty and clarity. The thing about this open communication is that there may be a lot of room for clashes of opinions and competition, so be on the lookout for that.

1 and 2

This is a warm relationship, but there's a chance it won't offer enough stimulation for either of you. Physical affection, support, trust, and being open and secure with emotional expression are hallmarks of this relationship. 1 takes the lead and is supported emotionally by 2. This is a lovely combination when dealing with the classic frameworks of husband and wife or employer and employee, although this doesn't mean the 1 and 2 combinations won't work in other forms of relationships. The important thing is that both parties are content to stay in their lanes. There's trouble in paradise when one decides to play a role outside of theirs.

1 and 3

These two are lovely for each other in terms of lighting a fire in their creative and imaginative endeavors and drives. This combination is full of inspiration, and there's never a dull moment for these two. In fact, there's a chance this could last a long time. The 3 is naturally open and affectionate, and this is something the 1 deeply appreciates. The 1 is a very driven person with a strong will, and this continues to inspire the 3. This is a lovely match indeed.

1 and 4

Usually, these two numbers don't mesh well with each other, at least not without a lot of love, understanding, and work. They both have very different viewpoints when it comes to life. However, this relationship has some serious gold to be mined within it because, as both parties have a very different approach to life, there are lots of lessons that can be learned that will help them stretch and grow in ways they could never have imagined if they were with someone more compatible. This doesn't mean you should go actively seeking this, but just know that if you do find yourself in this relationship, there's a lot of good even with the work. You should be aware that both numbers have a habit of not sharing their feelings, which means the emotional connection between both parties will leave a lot to be desired. The odds are this will become a source of frustration in the relationship, and, in the long term, things may not work out well. Don't just take the lessons you learned and move on.

1 and 5

1 has a strong will, while 5 has a free spirit. This seems like a match made in hell on the surface, but when both people actually put in the work to gain the other's affections, they can create a relationship that's vibrant, full of love and laughter. There's a chance that each partner will find it easy to offer the other the freedom they seek, and as a result, when they come together, it will always feel fulfilling. These two will find there's always something new to learn about each other, and this will keep the relationship going for a long time.

1 and 6

They have different ways of doing things, and yet they are huge fans of each other. There's a chance for them to build something that stands the tests of time and opposition, as long as they're each able to respect their different roles and respect each other. The 6 can be quite the nurturers, but they need to be careful about not nurturing the 1 to the point of over-mothering or "smothering" them because the 1 needs their space. Also, the 1 needs to make sure they make it clear how much they appreciate the 6. In other words, they both have to express their emotions clearly and with respect for the other person.

1 and 7

This match is an unlikely one, but it can offer loads of gifts for both parties when it does thrive. This relationship can become even richer when they choose to be understanding of each other. It's more likely than not going to be more platonic than romantic, being rooted more in the mind than the heart. The key here is to make sure they remain open and honest with each other. These two have common interests in information, history, and culture, and these pursuits can help the relationship remain interesting. If they don't have mutual interests, these two are likely to drift apart amicably.

1 and 8

"What happens when an unstoppable force meets an immovable object?" Well, this relationship is what happens. They are both dynamic and powerful numbers, and so when their worlds collide, you get fireworks. However, when it comes to the relationship, they're both domineering and assertive personalities, which may mean each person doesn't have enough room to thrive and be their best. Whether this relationship succeeds or not will come down to the willingness to compromise and offer each other enough attention, not just when it comes to work and goals but also in their personal lives. These numbers will need to learn humility and put in the work to keep their relationship alive.

1 and 9

These are at opposite ends of the numerological scale, and they can only do well together when they give each other space. They have mutual admiration for each other, but just like in the previous combination, they have to work to keep the relationship going while also not encroaching on each other's space. This relationship can be equal parts passionate and volatile.

1 and 11

This relationship will work out wonderfully well, just like with 1 and 2, except there will be double the insight and understanding here. The 11 is the visionary who gingers the 1's ambitions. However, it's important to maintain the very delicate balance of power here, particularly because of the 11's sensitivity. To thrive, these numbers have to see each other as equals.

1 and 22

As with 1 and 4, these two are going to need a lot of patience and hard work to succeed in a relationship with each other. The 1 needs to break new ground regularly, while the 22 brings twice the stability of the number 2, which could cause some frustration that ends the relationship before it's even had a chance to blossom. There are times when the 1 can drive the 22 in amazing ways, but this is the exception and not the rule.

2 and 2

This is a lovely pairing as no one could possibly understand a 2 like another 3. These people have no problem being very open with each other and offering themselves unconditional love and support. The stability and loyalty between these two are surreal. It's no Disney movie, but it is its own sort of magical. However, this pairing is not without its pitfalls because there's a chance that neither will have the chance to have the friction needed in relationships to help each other grow. In other words, it's not a match for those who value self-improvement.

2 and 3

These are very expressive partners, so this relationship will have love and passion in spades. Sometimes there may be flying tempers or colorful fireworks, but there's harmony rather than war for the most part. The 3s are easy-going and need to keep in mind that their second is very sensitive. Also, the two need to learn to express themselves in words whenever they feel their emotions or thoughts have been flippantly discarded or inadvertently disrespected by the three.

2 and 4

These could be a lovely pair. The 2 wants nothing more than loving commitment, and the four loves creating stability wherever they are; so this is a happy relationship. In fact, when these two meet and stop each other's breaths, there's a chance they'll get very serious very fast. However, it's almost like the 2 and 2 pairing in the sense that there may not be a lot of inspiration to be found here on account of the lack of friction. Perfect can become boring with time.

2 and 5

This pairing is a tricky one. The 5 wants nothing but to be free - and the 2 wants to connect. These are two different paths, and they will both feel very unfulfilled, having to deal with a lot of frustration over unmet needs. This means it's not likely that they can have a relationship that's beneficial to both of them. However, if they can find true love, there's a chance that the 5 can learn to be devoted and loyal, and the 2 can learn to let their 5 be free every now and then.

2 and 6

This relationship has potential. The 2 is emotionally sensitive; blending that with the 6's orientation toward family, this partnership can be full of understanding. However, the thing about any relationship with the two is that there's likely to be possessiveness and jealousy, and this is even more amplified with the 6. It makes sense when you consider that the 6 is very generous with their love. For this relationship to work, each side's need for personal space should be respected.

2 and 7

This combo can form a unique and lovely pairing when they're well-matched in a number of ways, and when they find these common threads they share, they can have a long-lasting relationship. These numbers lack nothing in the commitment department and are not afraid of things getting very deep to the point of having lasting love. They find a way to blend their hearts and minds beautifully well together.

2 and 8

These are among the most compatible pairs in numerology. The two bring emotional support and depth to the table, while the eight provides, which means they're both useful to each other. However, they both have to spend a fair bit of time getting to know the other person's unique traits because if they don't, they may take each other for granted, and their relationship may begin to feel like a steel cage.

2 and 9

People with these numbers are interesting together because they could either find it impossible to find their way out of the relationship with each other, or they could work toward becoming actual soul mates. They're both generous and compassionate, but the 9 exhibits these traits toward humanity as a whole, but not always toward the relationship. This could leave the two feeling very abandoned and hurt. Watching the 9 share their love with the world and not with them can be triggering for the 2, leading them to feel hurt and jealous. However, this can be fixed with affection and love within the relationship itself, leading to a romance that lasts with passion and intense affection.

2 and 11

This is a combination that could last forever. Just like with the 2 and 2, these two intuitively understand each other. The 11 is more likely to take charge in the relationship, acting as the elder or mentor, which works well for couples who find comfort in this dynamic.

2 and 22

This is a lovely combination that is similar to the 2 and 4, in that the 2 will find stability in the 22, and the 22 will find encouragement and emotional support from the 2. When these two fall in love, *they fall hard and fast.* The further along they go together, the more the 22 needs to be given space to interact with their spiritual side and not have to be the provider all the time.

3 and 3

What are you going to get with these two? Fun and chaos. The 3s are often attracted to each other right away, and they can inspire each other to lofty ideals, exciting each other at every turn. This is great if you're not looking for a long-term relationship, though, because the thing about 3s is that they're not stable, and there's hardly any commitment, at least not at first. This means that, before they know it, mundane living will get in the way, and what was once passion and fire will become boredom and exasperation. However, when these two are aware of this trait they have, they can have a love that lasts a lifetime.

3 and 4

This is a hard relationship. 3 is carefree and spontaneous, but 4 is careful and meticulous, so this will often cause issues for them both. The 3 can be quite the flirts and social butterflies, and this can make the 4 feel possessive and jealous, to the point of becoming controlling. The only way this can work for the long haul is if they make understanding each other their priority.

3 and 5

This couple is head over heels and enthusiastically into each other. They would also be awesome friends, constantly having adventures, laughs, and fun on their paths together. The thing is, they may both refuse to get into very serious conversations that need to be had, which means when problems rear their ugly heads, they're more likely to distract themselves and find ways to escape. If they both choose to work and commit to each other, there's a chance this could last a long time.

3 and 6

This is a lovely pairing that emphasizes family and social networking. They're both creative, which is a good thing. 6 is often the nurturer, making sure the relationship has all it needs for them to do well. If the 3 starts feeling a little too smothered or stifled, though, they may stray outside the bounds of their relationship and betray their partner. For this reason, 6 needs to let 3 be free. In turn, 3 needs to make sure they can give 6 the recognition and attention they need in the relationship.

3 and 7

This doesn't last a lifetime, but this pairing can defy the odds every now and then. When they find each other in love, it's an "opposites attract" situation. The 3 is caught in a flurry of social activity as usual, but the 7 desires nothing more than to enjoy their solitude. When the two can understand this about each other, and they choose to remain sensitive to their partner's opposing needs, they can do well together.

3 and 8

This is an unlikely pairing. The 3 are playful and creative, which means the materialistic and driven 8 may not get most of the time. There's, therefore, less of a chance for either one to do well in the relationship. However, there are times when they can find balance in their strengths and flaws, but that requires a lot of work, patience, and understanding.

3 and 9

These two are hard to miss in a crowd, and they always love impressing and intriguing each other. They have wisdom, passion, and creativity that keep things interesting and will make their relationship last for the long haul. However, they need to beware of financial matters and work as a team on this because finance isn't their strong suit and could be one of the major things that tear them apart.

3 and 11

This can be a successful relationship as with 3 and 2, with more depth, insight, and understanding. They're both intuitive and expressive, so as deep as their relationship can be, there's lots of fun to be had. However, 11 must take time to be on their own and recharge because they have different social needs than 3. Also, 3 needs to always remember that 11 is sensitive, even if they don't show it.

3 and 22

This one is very tough. 3 is carefree and spontaneous, but 22 is all about security and being able to see what's coming around the bend. These viewpoints can make it hard for them to coexist romantically, as they continue to feel misunderstood by each other. There can be times when the 22 funds the 3's talents and endeavors, but in the long run, this will not serve the 22 in a spiritual way.

4 and 4

This is a good match as they have the same goals and values, respect each other, understand how important order and stability are to each other and are willing to work hard for these values. They may butt heads every now and then, but their disagreements are just flashes in the pan that pass quickly. However, these partners may never be spontaneous or take risks, which means they can't have new experiences or grow.

4 and 5

These two numbers are very different temperamentally, which means they're not likely to be compatible. 5 wants to be free, but 4 wants to be stable and is looking for something for the long term. There's barely a chance these two will be able to give each other what they seek, which means a lot of unfulfillment within this relationship. The 5 will feel stifled, while the 4 will always feel anxious, never knowing if today is the day the 5 leaves for good.

4 and 6

This relationship is practical and offers the chance to have long-lasting bliss. They're practical, grounded in numbers, organized and dependable, and so this relationship will be firmly established on mutual trust, not romance and passion. They would have an even better relationship if they did their best to do something exciting every so often so that they didn't quickly get too comfortable and negligent.

4 and 7

A potentially great relationship, these numbers have traits that perfectly complement each other, yet they're different enough for things to remain interesting. There's a chance that their relationship may become more about intellectual and practical matters if they don't allow their hearts to open up to each other, so they need to fix that if they want this to last.

4 and 8

These are hard workers and great matches, who have the ability to plan for the long haul, and this brings the energy of reassurance, comfort, and stability, meaning they can both just enjoy each other with no worries. Practical issues are shouldered equally between the two, and they both feel like they're being treated equally and with respect. They just need to work on creating more of an emotional connection to make this a home run.

4 and 9

This relationship almost never happens, but it almost never lasts long when it does. The 4 is grounded and practical, which draws the 9 in because the latter tends to be quite unfocused. As the 9 remains open and relaxed, this teaches the 4 to ease up a little and not feel the need to have control over everything, going with the flow instead. If there's to be a deep connection here, that would depend on the other numbers in play with their numerology.

4 and 11

They are drawn to each other at first, but with time the 4 will find it hard to relate to the 11's spirituality, let alone share it since they're practical and very grounded. The 4 desires commitment, and the 11 can provide that. The 11 needs to feel safe, and 4 can give them that. However, 11 will eventually seek to break free, and it's not going to end well. If they both put in the work, though, they can learn a lot from each other, at least while they're still together.

4 and 22

These numbers are compatible as they have the same goals and values and therefore understand each other. However, the thing about master numbers is that at some point, they will have to be set free so they can explore their spirituality, and if the 4 doesn't give them the room to do this, the 22 will have to take it by force, or else there will be a world of resentment between these two.

5 and 5

These are twins that care about drama, adventure, and travel. They are aware of the need for them both to be free, and this means their partnership is advantageous for each other. They will never feel stifled or confined. There's a chance, though, that these numbers will completely ignore all the mundane things that, while "boring," are important to their relationship. They'd rather jump shop or distract themselves from the problem, so if this is going to be a long-term thing, they have to both commit and face the ugly as needed.

5 and 6

This is a relationship that can last, provided each party is open to making compromises. The 6 has a need for sanctuary and home, and that can clash with the 5's desire to be free. So, they both have to be very clear about what they need and how the other person can make that need happen, if at all they can. If they can make an agreement and hold up their end of the bargain, the relationship will flourish wonderfully.

5 and 7

There's so much potential with this pair. The 7 is fine with offering the 5 their freedom while they enjoy the stimulation and variety the 5 offers. In spite of them needing time apart, when they come together, sparks fly, oceans collide, and worlds are born. They just have to be willing to express their emotions as honestly as they can to keep this going.

5 and 8

This combo is a result of true admiration for one another, but there's not much to be had in terms of long-term commitment. This is due to the 8's desire for long-term commitment and structure, whereas the 5 is unwilling to have their freedom infringed upon in this manner. So, while there's a lovely dynamic between the two, it's not likely that they will make an effective team. When the love is strong enough, and they put in the work, making understanding front and center in their relationship. There's no height they can't attain together.

5 and 9

This couple is all about passion and adventure, and they can do well together when they give their "ship" enough energy and time. The only thing they need to be aware of is that their lives won't be intertwined enough to allow for a true emotional connection, so they need to be clear and open about what they want from each other.

5 and 11

This is a hard one. The 5s have to go exploring; the 11 needs to remain grounded and connected. That means they're not really suitable for each other. The 5 may think the 11 a little too intense. However, if the love they share is strong enough, it could work as long as the 11 has other connections that can feed their spiritual goals. However, this may not be enough to give depth to the relationship.

5 and 22

These have different temperaments, so they're very unlikely to go together. The 22 loves long-term commitment and stability, but the 5 isn't likely to offer that. They can mutually respect each other, but they're not likely to understand each other.

6 and 6

These twin numbers are very committed to each other, valuing creativity, health, family, and stability equally. They are intuitively in touch with each other's needs, and they can be amazing together when it comes to serving the world at large. However, they need to make sure they continue to maintain the balance in their home as well.

6 and 7

This can be tough, especially if partners aren't willing to compromise. The 6 may think the 7 is a tad too aloof for them, especially since they need some emotional certainty and control. However, if these numbers can try to be clear about what needs are going unmet with each other, and if they are both particular about making it happen, they could make it work.

6 and 8

This is a lovely combination that will do well in the long run if they both allow some compromise and put in the work. They're both very reliable and focused, which means they can have a love that lasts a lifetime. There can be trouble in paradise if they turn their docs on dissimilar interests, which is a possibility. The 8 might be more about their career and business, while the 6 may be more about the home and family, and this can be a problem if they don't take the time to understand how the other person has an equally important role and take an interest in the other's affairs.

6 and 9

This is a very fulfilling partnership for both parties. The 9 and 6 are idealistic, and they work hard too, so there's a chance they'll be able to meet each other's needs. They will have a powerful relationship when they're romantically connected, and this could last a lifetime.

6 and 11

This offers some mutual satisfaction. The 11 needs a safe base where they feel nurtured so that they can grow and explore their spirituality, and the 6 offers exactly that, which the 11 can see and appreciate. However, for this to last for long, the 6 needs to check their jealous emotions and exercise self-control so that the 11 isn't stifled in their development.

6 and 22

This is also a lovely relationship that can last a long time. They're both practical, grounded, and know how important it is to have a stable home. The ideal expression of this relationship has the 22 feeling secure enough to develop their spirituality, while the 6 understands how important their own role is as well, knowing the 22 doesn't take them for granted.

7 and 7

These are twins, so they *get* each other. This could be a deep and fulfilling relationship, and they both understand their desire to be alone and the other eccentricities they share. They are interested in each other, share their thoughts with each other, and explore their ideas and what they know. The trouble is, this number isn't the most grounded, so both of them will need to do their best to stay grounded each day.

7 and 8

This could work, but it may seem at first like these numbers have no business with each other. Where the 7 is more ephemeral and cautious in how they deal with things, the 8 is determined and a tad controlling. However, they can complement each other wonderfully and have a potentially long, rewarding relationship when they have other numbers lining up. They both have to make sure they remain emotionally open and that they're focused on more than just intellect and materialism so that they can get into the heart space and give the relationship solid ground to thrive on.

7 and 9

These numbers deeply appreciate each other and do not lack affection because their spiritual connection has remarkable depth. If they connect, there's a chance they're soul mates. If they aren't, the tension they experience being with each other will likely either gently challenge them to become better versions of themselves, keep them interested in the relationship, or have them part ways quickly. It all comes down to whether or not they will work to stay flexible and open when it comes to the other person.

7 and 11

This is like the 7 and 2, a unique blend, and if there are other commonalities with the other numbers you check them against, they can have a long life together. The 7 allows the 11 the space they need for spiritual growth, and the 11 will demonstrate how much they appreciate the 7 for partnering with them in this way. If the 7 doesn't give the 11 emotional closeness, this could become a serious problem.

7 and 22

A potentially good pairing like 4 and 7 would be ideal because they both have traits that beautifully complement each other and are different enough to keep things interesting. The 7 might become frustrated if they can't follow 22's schedule, but this is no cause for alarm because there's a chance these two will weather the storm and create a close, lasting relationship.

8 and 8

Being the same number means they understand each other. Success is equally important to this couple. This is a power couple, a prosperous one that can create the most lucrative, long-lasting business partnerships and marriages. The only issue here is that there's a risk of paying too much attention to work, to the point where the love and intimacy that *should* feed the relationship is missing. However, if they commit to keeping the flames alive, they will remain loyal to each other for a lifetime.

8 and 9

These are two strong numbers, both equally ambitious and determined, but they may have trouble connecting with each other because the 8 is more focused on power and money, while the 9 is more about humanitarian causes. The partnership may not last, or it could if they choose to see how they actually complement each other and learn from each other. It comes down to how much they want to make it work.

8 and 11

This is a pairing like the 8 and 2. 8 provides materially, and 11 offers emotional support and depth. They can be lovely together, but as time progresses, the 11 will need to pursue their spiritual goals, and this means they'll need space. If 8 can offer that, that would be great, and they could work together. However, it's not easy for these numbers to work out in a relationship because one person will definitely feel unfulfilled.

8 and 22

These two can work wonders when it comes to business and other matters. They love the security that comes with long-term plans and dealing with practical affairs, which allows them to grow in their personal lives. They can have a healthy and long-lasting marriage, and in fact, they make up a significant chunk of long-distance relationships, with them both being at ease with letting their partner have their space.

9 and 9

These two are the same, so they can last forever. They're both generous, passionate, and very happy with each other. They inspire other people in terms of relationship goals, and they bring a lot of good to the world.

9 and 11

These are a lovely pair as they're both generous and compassionate, but the thing about the 9 is that they share this love with one and all, and that could make the 11 feel like they're not being personally cared for and supported. Still, there's a chance that they both enjoy and appreciate being in the company of others and will allow each other the space to grow while having a safe space from which they can both come back and unite.

9 and 22

This is an unusual relationship that could lead to something lifelong. The 22 is practical and grounded. This is not only attractive to the 9 but also useful to them. The 22s are visionaries, and their insight will continue to offer intrigue and inspiration to the 9. 9 is fine with giving 22 the space they need to grow, but they have to make sure they're there to help the spiritual master with structure and support when they need it the most.

11 and 11

The connection between these two is deep. There is unconditional support, love, and compassion, which both partners desire and offer each other. They're fine with opening up about how they feel, and they have a healing effect on each other. It's very intense in this relationship, though, so it's a good idea for them to loosen up a bit, do pleasurable activities together, and seek friendships outside of themselves so they don't become recluses.

11 and 22

These are a powerful combination, both needing safety, connection, and depth, and both need to be able to provide the same to each other. They can be themselves with each other and completely relax. These numbers are loyal and committed, so there's nothing that can shake their love for each other. Also, when it's time for one or both to go after their spiritual development, there will be a lot of understanding and no hard feelings, keeping their bond intact forever. Together, they can create great change in the world.

22 and 22

They are very compatible when it comes to their needs and desires, knowing how to support each other. Both of them are intuitive and can connect quickly and deeply. Things will move fast between them when they fall in love. They'll be fine when it's time for one or both to go after spiritual matters, and they have the potential to transform the world incredibly.

Chapter 16: Add Numerology to Your Daily Life

In numerology, the idea that numbers are valuable and meaningful is a given. Understanding the numbers that make up our birthdays and names can provide a deeper understanding of what makes us unique, similar to the way in which astrology does. Using numerology in your daily life can assist you in the following ways:

- Recognize your own personal advantages and disadvantages
- Make a list of specific objectives for yourself
- Face the challenges that come your way with confidence
- Make the most of your interpersonal interactions
- Recognize the signs and affirmations of the divine all around you on a daily basis

Although the study of numerology may appear to be extremely complex, utilizing numerology to bring insight and clarity to your existence does not have to be as complicated as it appears. This chapter will show you a few straightforward methods to use numerology to make the most of your life.

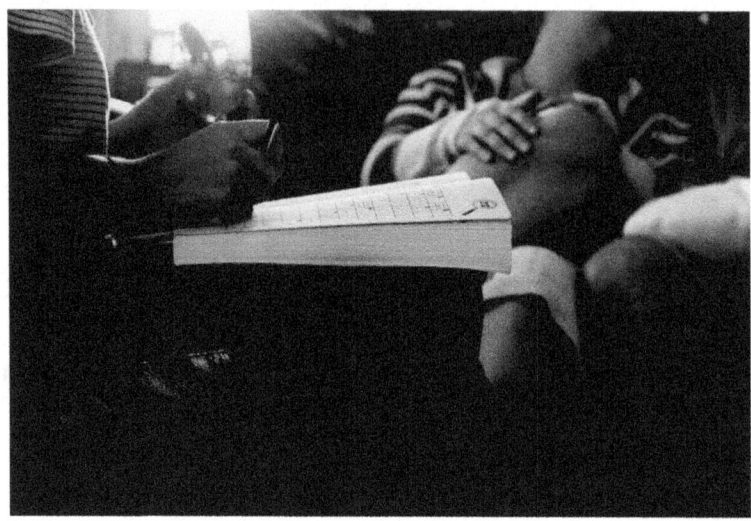

Numerology for Hiring Decisions

If you are a business owner or a manager of a company, you may have had the experience of looking for someone to hire and find yourself completely overwhelmed by the sheer number of excellent candidates for the job. The first thing you will have done, obviously, is to find out if their work experience is a match for the skill sets you require. You must have also taken a look at their qualifications, where they went to school, if they have any awards, and what their recommendations are. You may keep an eye out for professional bodies and associations or the things that they do in their free time, like volunteer work. You may have even made a few calls to their former employers to find out if they were great to work with. Now you have a shortlist that's really a long list and only one spot to fill.

Numerology can offer you a way to assess the character of the people you want to hire without needing to meet them face to face. Usually, when they apply, they'll have their date of birth on their resume and their full name, which should help you if you know enough about numerology. It's possible for someone to look very good on paper and still not be a great fit for your team. Since you know about numerology, you have an advantage when compared to other recruiters who have to sift through lots of meetings to make the right choice.

Making Good Investment Decisions

If you understand how to invest and make your money grow, that's one thing. You've handled all the technical, studied your charts, and learned all that you can about the companies that you think are worth backing with your hard-earned money. You may have tracked the performance of the CEO or chairman of a company and noticed that every time they take over a company, they tend to do extremely well. They could be all over the news on Bloomberg and CNBC as the "Person of the Year," and, for some people, that could be enough.

However, it would not be the first time someone who seemed to have integrity turned out to be nothing but a scam and fraud. They've had a long run of success, and it seems for a moment that they're doing fine until some dark and devious thing they did in the past comes to light, and that causes the stock of their company to crash. The odds are, if you had used numerology to look into them, you might have found something that would have kept you from investing your money with them. This is why, even after doing your homework with the more practical affairs, you should use numerology to suss out anything you might have missed or may not have seen in all your research. You can work with the names and birthdays of the CEOs to figure out whether or not they're worth your money.

- **Planning Out Your Life**

You can actually map your life out for the next nine years with numerology. Think of this as a forecast that helps you to figure out what's coming your way and how you can best prepare to mitigate the bad and take advantage of the good. There are many ways you can make these calculations. To make things simple, you can start by considering the date and month of each year in line with your personal numerology numbers.

The numbers indicate to you that, in certain months, you may be experiencing a lean period in finances. You can adequately prepare yourself to make sure you don't spend everything that you have. When it comes to your love life, if the predictions seem to indicate that there may be a rough period between you and your partner, you can begin to think about the things that you're dealing with or have yet to deal with and plan how best to address them going forward so that you can preserve the love you have. Numbers can be used to make life plans. Understanding how your personality is and how it works with others can help you take control of your life and make it a better one than you might have had alone. The types of relationships, financial decisions, and career paths that you choose can be based on the knowledge that numerology gives you about yourself.

- **Be Clear About Your Destiny**

Living life with no awareness of your destiny can be quite a scary and tumultuous experience. So, having learned such a powerful skill as understanding the energy of numbers, the first thing you should look at is what your destiny holds so that you can make sure that you're always in the right place at the right time and can take advantage of all opportunities that help you to actualize your greatness.

Since your habits form your character and your character drives your behavior, which leads to your destiny, you should understand what kind of character you have to take advantage of your strengths and mitigate the risks from your weaknesses. There's no better way to do this than by studying the numbers surrounding you. These numbers are an excellent way to learn about both your dark side and your good side so that you can see a trajectory of where you may wind up in the future, depending on which side you fuel.

- **Learning How to Train Your Kids**

As a parent, you naturally want the best life for your kids. You want to see them healthy and happy. As they grow older, you want them to succeed in whatever they decide to do. You send them to different classes to help them discover for themselves what they like and what they don't like. You encourage their dreams. You give them hope. However, as your life may have shown you over and over again, you know that success, happiness, and the good things in life are not necessarily a guarantee. You wish you could guide your kids right down the path that would be best for them, but how can you do that when you don't have a crystal ball? How can you be sure that you're raising them the right way and that you're not hurting them or their chances or their future?

By taking a look at the numbers in your child's life, you can learn a lot about who they really are and what would be best for them. The numbers can tell you about the negative and positive energies that they've taken on and how that will affect their character or behavior if you don't control it or help to hone it. When you have this information, you'll know what to do to help your child, and you'll be able to help them take better control of their not-so-great aspects so that they can do well for themselves in the future when you're no longer there to hold their hand.

- **Figuring Out Viable Business Partnerships**

Running a business means at some point in time, you might need a partner if you're going to take things to the next level. This partner will come in with the leverage and expertise you may not have. They could have a mouthwatering offer that makes it really difficult for you to refuse, and they may have an amazing track record as well. But the question is, does that guarantee you will find this partnership fulfilling?

You can use numerology to learn about your partner and see if they're compatible. Even though the compatibility we examined in the previous chapter is centered on love, here's the truth: the same things apply in business too. Make sure you evaluate your personal numbers and those of your potential clients, as well as the numbers attached to your business and theirs.

• Self-Upliftment

Numerology can be used to help you to understand your own personality and your strengths and weaknesses. Knowing your birth date can help you see how you react in different situations and find out if things are slipping through the cracks.

If you always seem a little overwhelmed under stress or feel like your impulsive traits get the better of you, studying your numerology might help you to better grasp certain hiccups in your life.

• Meeting New People

It is easy to spend time with only those you see as similar to yourself. If you know nothing about someone but they are a number of years or a week apart, there is a good chance that they have been through something similar to your own life, and that can be beneficial to you.

Finding out what their birth date means can help clarify why they may share certain traits with you. As you get to know them better, you can discover how the numbers in their name and birthdate relate to their personality.

• Understanding Your Purpose

Numerology helps us figure out why we are here on Earth, why we were created, and how we are going to live when we die. Knowing can help us make sure we're on the right path to becoming the grandest and best versions of ourselves. Every life has a purpose, and mastering our numerology can help us to find out more about that purpose. You may decipher your purpose by studying the unique attributes of your personality, the relationships in your life, and the decisions you have made throughout your life. All of these things are revealed by your numbers. Sometimes we know why we came here, and sometimes we don't. Numerology can help us figure out what the divine is trying to communicate through our name, thereby understanding how to fully express our authentic selves.

- **Practical Living and Better Self-Management**

As you spend more time learning what makes you unique, your life will be easier in various ways. You can manage your stress, realize why you might be impulsive, and make better decisions. The numbers are who we are; mastering their meanings and influences in *each part* of our lives will help us better manage ourselves *in all areas* of our lives.

- **Improving Relationships**

Your numerology information will also help you to master the relationships in your life. Learning the personality traits of others is important for happier and healthier relationships overall. You know right off the bat what your chances are with someone and whether you're willing to put in the work with them or not. Learning the numbers can also help to improve your relationships overall. You will be able to understand why certain people get on your nerves or become a source of stress in your life. Knowing what makes them tick will allow you to react in a more positive way, thereby helping everyone involved as time passes.

- **Financial and Career Success**

Some people excel above everyone else in every career; others seem to struggle just to make ends meet. Knowing your numerology can help you understand what makes you excel and what others do, which will help you make the best out of your career. As you start to gain more knowledge about numbers, your daily life will become easier. You get a lot of aha moments as you discover why stress might be a factor in making certain financial or career decisions or why you choose certain people as friends or associates. Knowing the numbers that matter will help you live a more fulfilling life.

- **Better Grasp of How People Think**

Numbers help us grasp why people think and react the way they do. You may find yourself in a situation where you cannot understand why an unruly child is throwing a tantrum or why an employee needs some encouragement from their boss. Knowing how the numbers affect their lives and what makes people tick will always be beneficial in daily life. You'll find yourself connecting better with others because of this, and they'll come to love you for it.

- **Finding Happiness**

To find happiness in life, we need to understand how we think and why we think the way that we do. Appreciating your personality traits and how they work with others will help you to find a more fulfilling life overall. Recognizing what makes you unique is an important part of every day, and your inherent uniqueness can be priceless. Numerology can show us why we are here on Earth, what our purpose is, why we need to make changes for the better, who our real friends are, and so much more about ourselves as individuals.

- **To Improve Your Mind and Make Better Decisions**

Figuring out what makes your mind tick, how it works, and why it works can help you be a happier and healthier person. Numerology is a factor in every aspect of life. Learning how others think and feel will help you improve your relationships, find happiness in life, and make better decisions. By recognizing the relevance of the numbers that define you, you will learn how you're perceived and present yourself so that you're less misunderstood. You will also be more aware of your cognitive biases and blind spots when the numbers show you your weaknesses. This makes you a better thinker. Numbers can show you why and how to make better decisions in life, allowing you to make the best of your time on Earth. You will be aware of what choices will give you the best overall results, and your personality traits will improve as time goes by.

- **To Improve Your Health**

Understanding what makes your body tick is a step towards bettering your life and making yourself healthier overall. Accepting how stress affects your body, how certain foods help or hinder it, and how these things affect your personality can help you make better decisions to improve the quality of your health and life.

- **How to Improve Your Life**

Knowing what makes us all want to work hard for our goals, be it money or success, is important. Working out why certain things or people motivate you and why others don't is equally important. Numbers, in general, and how they affect our lives on Earth, can truly help us acknowledge how we need to work on ourselves each day to improve ourselves physically, mentally, and emotionally.

Here's another book by Silvia Hill that you might like

Free limited time bonus

Stop for a moment. I have a free bonus set up for you. The problem is that we forget 90% of everything that we read after 7 days. Crazy fact, right? Here's the solution: we've created a printable, 1-page pdf summary for this book that you're reading now. All you have to do to get your free pdf summary is to go to the following website: **https://livetolearn.lpages.co/silviahill/**
Once you do, it will be intuitive. Enjoy, and thank you!

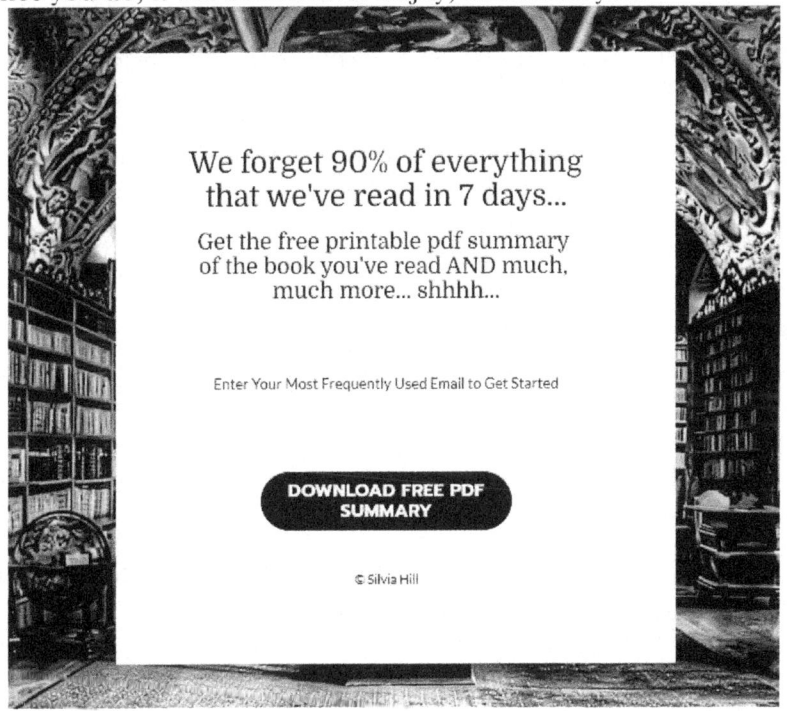

Index of Terms

Life Path — Reduced number of your birth date that dictates your life.

Destiny — Reduced number of all letters in your birth name that reveal your talents and gifts.

Master Number — Number with the most powerful positive and negative traits. Often, double digits need not be reduced. 11, 22, 33 are master numbers.

Power Number — Other double-digit numbers besides 11, 22, and 33.

Karmic Debt Number — Number representing your lesson for this lifetime.

Birthday Number — Number based on your date of birth that offers insight into your character and luck.

Growth Number — Shows you the path to advancing in life.

Destiny Number — Shows your hidden skills and talents, as well as a trajectory in life.

Soul Urge Number — Reveals your inner desires and driving forces

Personality Number — Shows your kind of person and how you interact with others.

Heredity Number — Shows the familial forces that affect your life going back generations.

References

Abraham, Karin Lee. Healing Through Numerology. 1st ed. Euclid, Ohio: RKM Publishing Co., 1985.

Balliet, Mrs. L. Dow. Number Vibration in Questions and Answers. 2nd ed. Albuquerque, New Mexico: Sun Publishing Co., 1983.

Eisen, William. The English Cabalah, Volume I, The Mysteries of Pi. 1st ed. Marina del Rey, Calif.: DeVorss and Company, 1980.

Guthrie, Kenneth Sylvan, comp. And trans. The Pythagorean Sourcebook and Library. Grand Rapids, Mich.: Phanes Press, 1987.

Javane, Faith, and Dusty Bunker. Numerology and the Divine Triangle.

Kline, Morris. Mathematics and the Search for Knowledge. New York: Oxford University Press, 1985. Kozminsky, Isadore. Numbers, Their Meaning, and Magic. York Beach, Maine.

Oliver, George. The Pythagorean Triangle, or The Science of Numbers. San Diego: Wizard's Bookshelf, 1984.

Wilson, Hazel. A Guide to Cosmic Numbers. Foibles Publications, 1982